Gypsy Days on the Delta

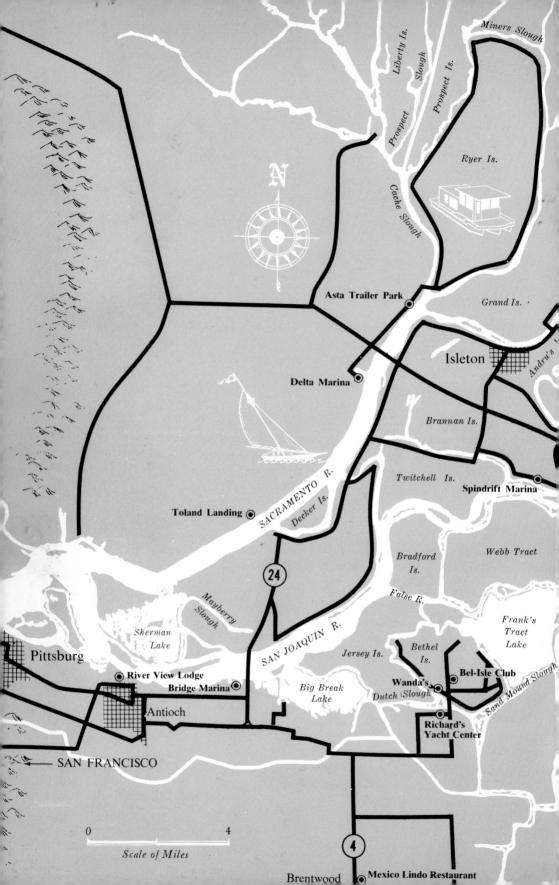

Miners Slough

Liberty Is.

Prospect Slough

Prospect Is.

Ryer Is.

Cache Slough

N

Asta Trailer Park

Grand Is.

Isleton

Andru's I.

Delta Marina

Brannan Is.

SACRAMENTO R.

Twitchell Is.

Spindrift Marina

Toland Landing

Decker Is.

Webb Tract

(24)

Bradford Is.

False R.

Frank's Tract Lake

Mayberry Slough

SAN JOAQUIN R.

Sherman Lake

Jersey Is.

Bethel Is.

Bel-Isle Club

Pittsburg

Wanda's

Sand Mound Slough

River View Lodge

Big Break Lake

Dutch Slough

Bridge Marina

Antioch

Richard's Yacht Center

← SAN FRANCISCO

0 — 4

Scale of Miles

(4)

Brentwood   **Mexico Lindo Restaurant**

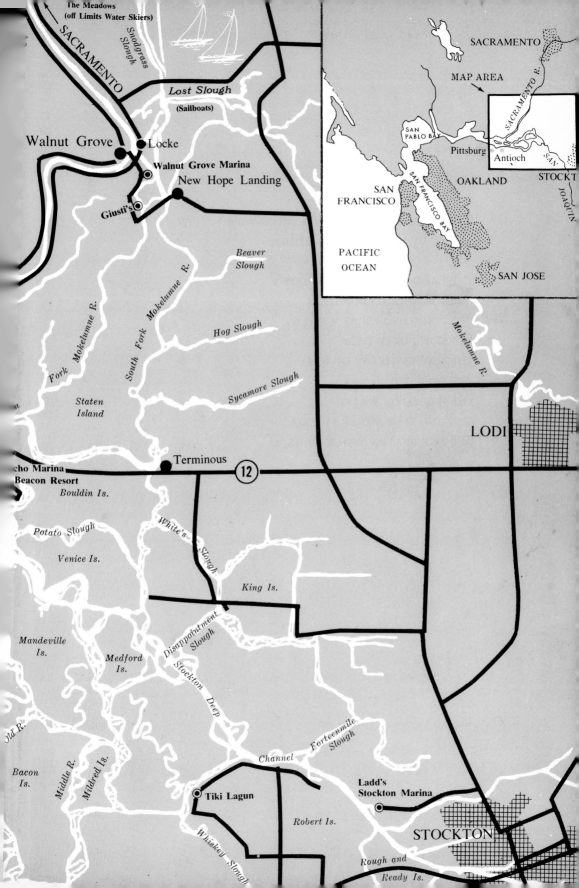

In the wake of the River Queen.

Gypsy Days on the Delta

ERLE STANLEY GARDNER

William Morrow & Company, Inc.
New York 1967

Contents

Color photographs appear after page 192

List Of Illustrations

Acknowledgments

So many people help me with these Delta books that it is impossible to make individual acknowledgments. Suffice it to say that the people in and around Bethel Island and on the Delta are some of the nicest, most hospitable, helpful people I have ever met.

For the photographs in this book, I am deeply indebted to Jean Bethell, who took some of both color and black and white; to Richard DeShazer, who is a wonderful photographer and who always puts his color shots at my disposal; and to Sam Hicks, who has taken many of the pictures which I use from time to time in my books.

ERLE STANLEY GARDNER

The River Queen moored under shade trees.

CHAPTER ONE

Mixed Inheritance

As a yachtsman, I am a nautical landlubber.

On my father's side I am descended from hardy New England stock. My forebears were the captains of windjammers, whalers which went out of Nantucket and remained for many months, clippers which raced to China and sailed the Seven Seas.

My dad always loved the water. The more it stormed, the better he liked it. He loved to feel a good stout deck quiver and shake beneath his feet as some heavy ocean roller shook the boat from stem to stern. At such times all the atavistic memories of prior incarnations of fearless sea captains would come to the front and he would stand braced against the wind, the salt spray hurtling past him, a look of keen enjoyment in his eyes.

My mother always got seasick.

I take after my mother.

Perhaps that is an oversimplification. My stomach takes after my mother.

Actually, I am a weird combination of mother and father. I love the water. I love adventure. I love the thrill of sailing to strange lands, of coming in to foreign ports, of seeing exotic

I love to see exotic dancers.

dancers. The sight of a sailing ship with canvas spread in the sunlight calls to something in my blood which I can never fully understand.

On the other hand, when the waves become stronger and smash against the boat, when the good ship starts creaking and groaning in the midst of a storm, I chicken out.

On such occasions I get below deck. I saturate myself with all the latest remedies for seasickness and some that are more old-fashioned. None of them works.

I am an expert on seasickness.

My father's adventuring spirit causes me from time to time to accept invitations which are given me by yachtsmen to go on long cruises on some deluxe yacht. This same spirit of adventure also causes me to scorn the airplane when it comes to crossing the ocean. I want a good staunch ship. I want to feel the tang of the salt breeze.

So I go on ships.

Then I get seasick.

2

Because I have specialized in seasickness, I have a scorn for the dilettante individual who mistakes nausea for seasickness.

Many times I have heard persons describing some spell of "seasickness." I have asked them in great detail about the symptoms.

When they get done, I shake my head condescendingly and say, "You weren't seasick, you were nauseated."

I always start out on my ocean trips in high spirits. The blood of my paternal ancestors sees to that. The smell of caulking is aroma to my nostrils. The hint of adventure ahead is manna to my soul.

I always arrive in low spirits.

The boat gets me there despite my frequent desire to jump overboard and swim back.

As a result, I have sailed the Seven Seas and can talk about Hong Kong, Manila, the Sulu Archipelago, the Mediter-

My present fleet of boats moored where there is no chance of the owner getting seasick.

ranean, the mysterious South Sea Islands, and the lure of the Orient.

I have also been on yachts. My friend, Adolph G. Sutro of San Francisco, invited me to cruise on a forty-two-foot yacht from San Francisco to Alaska.

I accepted.

This was a real nautical yacht. My friend had purchased it in New Bedford and had it shipped out as deck load on a freighter. This helped give me a professional background. When we would tie up in some place such as Bodega Bay and I would go ashore, the inhabitants would see that I had disembarked from a forty-two-foot yacht named "SPRAY—New Bedford." They would look at me with awe, never suspecting my cruise had actually begun in San Francisco Bay.

I accepted their adulation. After what I had been through I felt I was entitled to it.

We cruised to Alaska in installments. It consumed my vacation time for two years to get the yacht to Tillamook, Oregon; then I joined my friend by train and we made a mad dash to the north.

Yo heave ho, and a bottle of rum!

We got in a storm off the coast of Oregon which was one of

Most people relax on the high seas.

I am a wonderful fair-weather sailor.

the worst storms the Pacific Northwest had ever seen. We were in the middle of it, clawing off shore, with great logs from broken-up logging booms caught on the crest of breakers and whizzing past us in the darkness like huge missiles projected by some giant hand.

If one of those logs had struck us head on, our boat would have been smashed to kindling wood.

I couldn't have cared less.

My friend had two hunting dogs with him. These dogs were hoisted ashore at available wharves, then put back aboard at the end of a rope. The dogs were very much with us during the storm.

The dogs became seasick.

When a dog becomes seasick, he isn't simply nauseated, he is seasick.

I have sailed the seven seas and can talk about foreign lands . . .

. . . especially the South Seas . . .

. . . and South Sea dancers!

There were two tiers of bunks on each side of a narrow cabin. I had a three-foot board which fitted into grooves on the outer side of the bunk so that the violent motion would not throw me out. I braced myself against this board on one side, the wall of the ship on the other.

The dogs were down on the linoleum floor. When the boat would roll they would try to dig in with their claws to keep from rolling with the boat. The effort, of course, was in vain. The claws would make a scraping sound along the linoleum. Then there would be a series of two thuds as the inert bodies would slam into the drawers which were below the bunks on each side of the cabin.

Spray *was a real nautical yacht.*

The boat would then roll to the other side. The dogs would try to hold themselves with their claws. There would be the same noise of scratching, then the thud of two bodies against the drawers on the other side.

In the meantime, the dogs were just as seasick as I was, and, although long since rid of any food in their stomachs, continued to retch and water at the mouth.

A particularly violent wave threw me clean over the top of the three-foot board and I dropped, an inert mass, to the floor below.

Fortunately, I missed the dogs.

From then on, the three of us lay on the floor and tried to brace ourselves against the roll of the boat.

Our attempts were in vain.

The dogs' claws dug into the linoleum and scraped. My

fingernails dug into the linoleum and scraped. As the boat would finish its roll to one side, there would be three thuds instead of two.

I was also slobbering and retching, but the time had long since passed when any real regurgitation was possible. Now and then a few teaspoonfuls of bitter bile would burn my stomach, corrode my throat, and add to the mess on the floor.

The dogs didn't have the strength or the will to get up. I didn't have the strength or the will to get up.

Eventually, the boat arrived in Puget Sound. I recuperated somewhat. We cruised Puget Sound and enjoyed the magnificent scenery, and after returning to the calm waters of Seattle, I blossomed out in a gold-braided yachting cap, some ice-cream trousers, and a blue serge double-breasted coat with brass buttons.

I looked the part of an adventuring yachtsman.

The big Airedale "Rye" being lifted ashore.

We returned to San Francisco. My vacation time was up. We had cruised to the Puget Sound. We had not reached Alaska. My friend, Sutro, is a determined individual. He said, "We will go to Alaska. Next year we will ship the yacht to Seattle and start from there. Since we have already sailed that distance, it won't be cheating to start from there next year."

The yacht was rigged for sail. We had experienced quite a bit of trouble with the gasoline "kicker." I pointed out that the swift tide currents and narrow channels of the Inside Passage were deadly for a sailboat. We needed a motor cruiser for the Alaskan trip.

Sutro is determined. In fact he has a streak of obstinacy in his makeup. He said, "I will completely remodel the boat and put in the biggest, heavy-duty gasoline motor money can buy; but we are taking this boat to Alaska!"

Sutro put in eight months remodeling the boat. The next summer we shipped it to Seattle by deck load on a freighter and from that vantage point we cruised to Alaska and back.

Puget Sound and the Inside Passage . . .

. . . offer magnificent scenery.

When I wasn't seasick, I put on my yachting togs and went ashore and had pictures taken. People read the registration on the yacht's stern and assumed we had sailed it all the way from New Bedford.

Who was I to contradict them?

The editor of one of the yachting magazines looked at me in awe when we met him. He was sure that his readers would like to hear an account of our daredevil trip.

I told him I would write an account only if I could tell the truth, that I was convinced yachting stories frequently departed from the truth.

The editor wanted to know how and why.

I told him that in my limited experience of reading yacht-

Fishing shacks of the Alaskan Indians.

ing stories, I found they usually started with the narrator having an argument with the "captain." The author insisted that it would be raining by midnight and the captain, studying the "glass," would insist that there was no chance of rain. (All this was long before portable television and hourly radio broadcasts on the weather.)

The story would go on to tell how the author was awakened by the pattering of rain on the roof of the cabin. He aroused himself sufficiently to look at his watch. The time was exactly one minute to twelve.

I told the editor I couldn't write this kind of a story, that it wouldn't be true; that I would write a plain, unvarnished account of my adventures in sailing to Alaska.

The editor said that was exactly what he wanted.

I wrote the story.

No one believed it.

I told the simple, unadulterated truth about our trips, and the story was considered the greatest flight into the fields of maritime humor that any magazine had ever published.

The editor ran it in three installments with copious photographs, and yachting circles ate it up. The editor told me afterwards it was by far the most popular serial the magazine had ever published. Everybody read that story and laughed themselves sick. They thought it was satire, burlesque, fictionalized fact.

I called it "The Log of a Landlubber."

A few years later an elaborate expedition was being planned to cruise down the peninsula of Baja California and around the Cape of San Lucas into the Sea of Cortez.

Because I was considered a ripsnorting yachtsman, I was invited to bring my friend, Dr. E. K. (Dusty) Roberts, the noted archer, and join the expedition.

We shipped the remodeled boat to Seattle.

Among some of the celebrities who were going on the cruise would be the commodore of one of the most exclusive yachting clubs on the coast. Anita Haskell Jones, who held a woman's world's record for catching marlin on light tackle, would be along; so would her brother, her sister, and her brother-in-law. A powerful figure in the business world would be taking the cruise, and also a chain-restaurant owner.

It was a huge yacht. As I remember it, the mainmast was a hundred and sixty-odd feet high. The yacht was over a hundred and twenty-five feet in length.

The whole cruise was to be a super deluxe affair, and "Dusty" Roberts and I would have the opportunity of hunting in ports which had never been hunted by anyone and killing deer and antelope with bow and arrow.

We were to stop in places where there were no ports, anchor the boat, and go ashore in powerboats. We were to explore virgin islands. We were to see things no other yachtsmen had ever seen.

The blood of my father influenced my judgment. I accepted the invitation.

On boarding the yacht, I found that the hard-bitten yachtsmen who were taking the cruise were all impressed by the extent of my maritime experiences. They had all read "The Log of a Landlubber" and thrilled to its humor, its sheer hyperbole. They looked in awe upon a man with such vivid imagination that he could conjure up a bewildering array of landlubberly experiences which supposedly had taken place on a single yachting trip.

I accepted their adulation, extracting all the enjoyment possible from a situation which was completely foreign to me.

Equipped in my natty yachting costume, I joined the yachtsmen aboard the boat at the dock. I strolled the deck,

Totem pole.

14

Anita Haskell Jones . . .

pausing now and then to regard parts of the boat with what the bystanders took to be an experienced eye. I let Anita Haskell Jones have her picture taken with me. I took pictures of her. As a hard-bitten, veteran yachtsman, I tried not to be patronizing.

We were to start at dawn, but with the dawn came one of those terrific windstorms which suddenly sweep Southern California. Small-craft warnings were up, and, while we went to the outer harbor, we couldn't get out into the tumbled mass of whitecaps which we could see through the binoculars.

The yacht-club commodore who was in charge of operations was impatient.

I was impatient. The blood of my forefathers demanded

16

that we go out and meet the elements head on, man against nature, a staunch boat, a yo-heave-ho and a derring-do!

It was getting along in the afternoon. There was a great deal of impatience. The commodore deferentially put it up to me. What did I think of it? The wind had gone down a little, but the question was would it come up again that night? We had a hundred and umpty feet of staunch yacht beneath us which was entirely different from the ordinary type of small boat. There was a chance that . . .

I interrupted him impatiently, "What was the problem?"

He pointed toward the tumbled mass of churning water, raised his voice so that it was audible above the whistling of wind in the rigging. What did I think of the storm?

I gave him a cold eye. "What storm?"

"Why, the storm outside."

"A sailing breeze," I said, and turned away.

That did it. The commodore and his bully boys rallied to the siren call of adventure. We cast loose and headed out into the churning waste.

. . . served her watch at the wheel.

When we got there, the waves looked much bigger than they had through the binoculars, but I stood swaying on the deck, my arms folded, a glint of disdain in my eyes.

People looked at me with admiration. I was the typical hard-boiled yachtsman—New Bedford to San Francisco, San Francisco to Alaska. Batten down the hatches and to hell with the storm!

Then I began to feel unduly warm. A cold perspiration enveloped my skin. The saliva formed in my mouth a little faster than I could swallow, but I swallowed as rapidly as possible, knowing with each swallow that this was the wrong thing to do.

There was some sort of a bedraggled paint bucket in what I would refer to in a yachting story as the "scuppers."

The sight of that bucket had triggered a whole series of emotional and physical reactions. Suddenly I felt a major earthquake on a scale of about Richter 8 taking place in my

L. to R.: Henrietta Sutro (Adolph's mother), Arlyn C. Peterson, Adolph G. Sutro.

The yacht said we were from New Bedford. Who was I to contradict such a statement?

stomach, with the epicenter just above the liver. I made a dive for the bucket.

I started for the cabins. The motion of the boat tripped me. Down the companionway I went, bucket and all, head over heels, nausea over misery.

Moaning, I took my whimpering hulk into my stateroom, clutched the bucket in my arms, and passed from nausea to extreme nausea, from extreme nausea to seasickness.

No one saw me until daylight the next morning when our bedraggled boat put into the calm harbor at Ensenada.

True to form, I had been transported in misery to another exotic port.

I was living up to my billing.

Later on, I distinguished myself in a nautical argument.

The commodore had anchored in a wide bay. He painstak-

Anita Haskell Jones and the owner of the yacht, "Laz" Lippman, had read my yachting story and were impressed by my nautical experience.

ingly started to give me a lecture on navigating from a chart.

"We are right here," he said, "where I have made this cross on the chart. I know where we are because the chart shows a twin peak—and you can see the twin peak right over there. Now I take a compass bearing on that twin peak, then I take a cross bearing on that butte—and here we are!"

"Wait a minute," I said. "How do you know that so-called twin peak isn't two peaks almost in line? Why isn't that the twin peak over there? And as for a cross bearing on that butte, there are half a dozen buttes."

I warmed to the subject as I saw a look of doubt coming over the face of the commodore.

At that time, I was a pretty fair lawyer. I was always a poor yachtsman—so I gave the guy a break. "Don't let me convince you," I warned. "I know little about charts, but I'm an expert at argument."

That much warning I gave him, and then I went to work.

I "sold" the guy. He ordered up the anchor, took my interpretation of the chart and moved over to *my* interpretation of the landmarks.

A few minutes later when we were hard aground, I said, "Commodore, what does the chart show?"

He said, "The chart shows that if we had been where you said we were, we wouldn't be where we are now. Go below and stay there!"

That is the trouble. I argue better than I sail.

It was a long trip and, after that, the commodore and I exchanged very few words—and those words were *not* on nautical subjects.

CHAPTER TWO

What Is Seasickness?

Fortunately, very few people have really experienced seasickness.

Nausea is, of course, a preliminary symptom, but it is no more indicative of seasickness than a chill and fever is indicative of malaria. It is what might be called an indispensable symptom, although I understand there are persons who claim to have become seasick without the nausea.

I regard this with a large slice of doubt.

At one time, on the Alaskan trip, it became necessary to anchor the boat in a small cove and put me ashore for twenty-four hours. I had become so nauseated that in between spells of retching my body muscles would be seized with cramps which would tie them in knots. Running a hand over my body, my torso felt like a sack of potatoes. The pain, of course, was excruciating.

I have an idea I would have died if I hadn't been put ashore to recuperate.

At the end of twenty-four hours of blissful rest, I had to get back aboard that damn yacht. There was no other way of leaving the place.

There is no form of adventure quite like that to be found in a yacht.

I was supercargo on a freighter . . .

My friend, Louis Roripaugh, for many years the manager of the Vail Ranch at Temecula, has given me a very vivid description of people suffering from seasickness.

The Vail Company was one of California's big cattle ranching empires. It owned a tract of ninety-six thousand acres contiguous to my own modest holdings in Temecula.

The Vail family also owns the Santa Rosa Island, one of the so-called Channel Islands off Santa Barbara. This island is roughly sixty-four thousand acres—or ten miles square. The Vails ran many hundred head of cattle on this island, maintaining their own boat which sails back and forth from Santa Barbara or San Pedro.

From time to time, they had to transport cowpunchers over to the island, and many of these cowpunchers were Mexican nationals.

For some reason it would seem that the Mexicans are somewhat more prone to seasickness than the other cowpunchers.

Louis was telling me the story of transporting five Mexican cowpunchers over to the island. They had started in the eve-

. . . which took a deck load of lumber through the Canal to New York.

We chartered this boat on a moment's notice . . .

ning, had run into a storm, and were being tossed around like a cork during the long, wind-whistling night hours.

In the morning, Roripaugh couldn't find the five Mexicans. He started looking for them with some alarm.

Finally he found them.

His description is indicative of what happens when a person gets seasick. Louis has something of a cowboy drawl and a natural picturesque speech which is the result of having been in the cattle business all his life.

"I found those five Mexicans in a human ball down in the lowest part of the boat," Louis said. "They were all tangled up like a bunch of angleworms in the bottom of a tin can, and *everything* had happened to them which could *possibly* happen."

Judging from Louis' vivid description, I am inclined to think these five Mexicans were seasick.

Despite my seasickness, however, the fact remains that there is no form of adventure quite like that to be found on the ocean.

Early in my writing career when I wanted to go to New York, I had a chance to ship on a freighter as supercargo. I grabbed at the chance.

It was a slow boat with a deck load of lumber, and we sailed majestically down the west coast of California, Mexico, and Central America, through the canal, and up to New York. I was an unable-bodied seaman on the trip.

I remember that several years ago a small party of us set out in two cars to drive over the Alaskan Highway.

We started during what turned out to be the most dusty season of the year. The road was a mass of dust. Everything

. . . and cruised Puget Sound.

we had became coated with dust—cameras, sleeping bags, provisions, suitcases, hats, eyes, ears, noses, and mouths.

We were all dust!

After a few hundred miles, we held a meeting. The consensus of the meeting was "to hell with it." We'd find a vacation somewhere else.

We turned around and headed for Vancouver. We had no plans. We simply wanted to get away from that eternal problem of dust. We wanted to find some place where we could get a good hot bath, break out some clean clothes, and lick our lips without making a mud pie in our mouths.

Once we arrived in Vancouver, we had no place we really wanted to go except Puget Sound, so we started looking for a boat which could be chartered.

Eventually we found a boat and, on a moment's notice, so to speak, we were loading the thing helter-skelter with provi-

L. to R.: Sam Hicks, "Les" Bethell, and Frank Orr.

Enjoying the scenery.

sions and heading out on a cruise with our destination unknown.

Puget Sound is not generally as rough as the outer ocean.

I had, of course, on my trip to Alaska traversed the two really rough places which are a nightmare to the yachtsman —Dixon's Entrance and Queen Charlotte Sound.

The adventures we had on that impromptu Puget Sound yachting trip have become gems in memory's storehouse and, yet, recounting those adventures makes them seem highly prosaic.

There was the time when we put into port to wait out a storm. We found it was a port favored by tugboat captains who had logging booms in tow and ran for this shelter when it became necessary to wait out a "blow."

It was a little seaport catering only to boat crews, and out

We dug clams and had barbecues ashore.

on the end of the wharf was a restaurant presided over by a motherly woman who kept ample supplies of apples, sugar, flour, shortening, etc. Whenever it really started to blow she started making apple pies.

She had found that the tugboat captains, in a savage mood because of the weather and the lost time, would be solaced by piping-hot slices of thick, juicy apple pie with flaky piecrust—the top sprinkled with cinnamon, the hot apples exuding a buttery syrup which, mingling with a scoop of ice cream, would cause anyone to forget his troubles.

By the time we returned to Vancouver we had had a real vacation.

31

I have always had a weight problem. Up until I was thirty, I was too skinny, and then suddenly the huge doses of cod-liver oil and malt syrup began to take effect all at once and I started having the other side of the problem.

However, I threw all dietary precautions to the wind once we found out that this woman was baking a steady output of apple pies. We simply tied our boat up to this wharf, and my diet for the next thirty-six hours consisted primarily of apple pie à la mode—a nearly continuous stream of savory calories.

I don't know about the tugboat captains but, personally, I saw that storm let up and the wind go down with mingled feelings. I wanted to continue our adventure, but I also wanted to keep on eating apple pie à la mode.

After that we just went places in Puget Sound—fishing from time to time, exploring little out-of-the-way ports, or just cruising along, propped against a backrest with binoculars, studying the shore and watching the wildlife.

Money invested in a yacht yields more relaxation than any other similar investment.

There are thousands of boats in the Delta.

By the time we returned to Vancouver, we had had a real vacation.

I have always wanted to go over the Alaskan Highway, but I know instinctively that if I ever try again I will get a couple of hundred miles up the highway, then turn abruptly and race back to Vancouver, charter a yacht, and again explore the Puget Sound country—particularly if I have a captain who has sense enough to listen to me when I tell him that, if he values his boat, he had better put into a protected port when the wind starts to come up.

Throughout the country we have opportunities for maritime enjoyment which offer wonderful possibilities for adventure and recreation. In Southern California there is San Diego Bay with the nearby islands and the hospitable shores of Baja California; Ensenada with its beautiful Todos Santos Bay;

The marina at Walnut Grove.

the new marina at Oceanside; Balboa and Newport Harbor and their wonderful yacht clubs and anchorages; the relatively nearby island of Catalina, the marinas at Ventura and Santa Barbara; the Channel Islands.

Anyone who is a good sailor, fortunate enough to live along the West Coast of the United States, will find that dollar-for-dollar money invested in a yacht will give him more relaxation, more thoroughgoing enjoyment, more health, more peace of mind than any similar investment he can make.

However, when one is half sea captain and half chicken, he is presented with a problem.

I wrestled with this problem until suddenly I found the ideal spot for a landlubber with nautical ideas—the Delta region of California.

When one cruises the Delta region and sees the thousands and thousands of boats docked along the shores in the various

34

marinas, he feels that everyone in the world has discovered this haven.

But when he starts out on the tranquil waters which are referred to locally as "a thousand miles of inland waterways," he realizes that he is in a veritable boating paradise. And considering the proximity of Sacramento, Stockton, Antioch, Oakland, Alameda, Berkeley, and the cities of the North Bay congested with people who certainly must be tired of the bumper-to-bumper problems of so-called recreation by auto-mobile, the Delta is still relatively undiscovered territory.

My own introduction to the Delta country came in a typical way.

I had a hideout in the State of Washington on the Hood Canal. I brought up a nineteen-foot boat with twin outboards, and we explored during calm weather. But I wanted to get back into the majestic scenery of Puget Sound so, during a period when my father's blood was surging through my veins,

My cruiser, the Gineva, *in Puget Sound.*

I bought a very fine cruiser—one which was specially designed for cruising in that type of water.

Then a series of circumstances made the Washington property a little too remote from my center of operations. We got up there only infrequently during the summer and, when we were there, had little occasion to use the boat.

I learned that I could ship the boat south by truck, and looked for some central location where I could keep it to advantage and use it from time to time.

As soon as I started studying the map, I discovered the Delta region.

So I had the boat shipped down to Antioch, had it overhauled and made ready for cruising.

It soon became apparent, however, that this boat—while ideal for the Puget Sound country—was not the best boat in the world for the relatively shallow waters of the Delta region.

I could cruise in the main channels with the greatest of

It behooves the navigator to consult a tide table when he moors his boat.

A portion of Dick DeShazer's Yacht Center.

comfort, but when it came to exploring little side passages or going into secluded anchorages, the draft of the boat presented a problem causing ever present concern.

Despite the fact that for the most part the water in the Delta is fresh, it is still pushed up and down by the tidal thrust of the waters surging in from the Golden Gate, and a boat which is floating peacefully when one goes to bed at night may be high and dry in the morning with the receding tide.

The big danger, however, is running aground in some shallow anchorage during a period of high tide, waiting out the tide, only to find that the next high tide is lower and the next high tide even lower than that.

On the other hand, as soon as I hit the Delta country I realized that I had found the ideal place as far as I was con-

The River Queen leads the way up the river.

cerned. The adventuring spirit of the blood of my father's ancestors would enable me to enjoy yachting, yet I would never be out of sight of land. My cruising would be on waters which might perhaps—in their more open stretches and at the height of winter storms—induce nausea, but could never become so violent as to cause seasickness.

While we had our deep-sea cruiser anchored, I saw house cruisers floating past and suddenly decided that my transportation was somewhat out of place.

So I told my friend, Bill Abell—a mechanic who had been putting the boat in shape and showing me some of the choice fishing grounds in the Delta country—that I wanted to look into the houseboat situation.

Bill promptly got me in touch with Roland Ayo, who is a salesman for Richard DeShazer, who owns Richard's Yacht

Center and is one of the really big yachting brokers in the area.

Ayo had assured me that they would make some sort of a trade and take my cruiser in on either a houseboat or a house cruiser. Everyone recommended a house cruiser for the type of work I had in mind.

The house cruiser is now coming into its own. It has abandoned the scowlike bow which was typical of the houseboat, and it is powered with a thoroughly adequate series of motors which give it a first-class performance.

I listened to Ayo and DeShazer. I took my first ride in a house cruiser, a single-engined River Queen with a steel hull.

And, suddenly, I knew I had found exactly the form of recreation I wanted.

The River Queen, the Whit-Craft, and the Valco cruiser tied up below a drawbridge.

39

Since that time, I have, of course, graduated. I have become a Delta fan deluxe. I now have two house cruisers—a River Queen and a Whit-Craft. The original single-motored River Queen has been traded in on a twin-engined later model River Queen house cruiser which has an electric generator sufficiently powerful to be a localized power plant.

This boat has an electric refrigerator, an electric range, electric water pump, electric water heater, hot and cold running water—even a refrigerated air-conditioning unit. The Whit-Craft is a somewhat smaller, more compact edition with a generator, electric kitchen, refrigerator, and shower.

This Whit-Craft makes an ideal companion for the River Queen because when I cruise I have to take my office with me.

Last year Dick DeShazer and his wife, Moyne, went cruise-camping with us. I also had two secretaries and Sam Hicks along. We established a portable field office and enjoyed the Delta while I kept up with the most important part of my work.

Dick and Moyne DeShazer went camping with us.

Jean Bethell.

I wrote up that trip in my book, *The World of Water.**

Because I have a steady stream of book royalties coming in, as well as an interest in television, I am financially able to live as I would like to live in the Delta country.

Because I have these same interests, however, I have to keep in almost daily touch with my office and, every few days, I must pick up mail.

This tends to complicate my own cruising problems. On the other hand, the income is sufficient to enable me to keep a fast cruiser and an eighteen-foot work boat in which to run back and forth with mail.

The fact remains that I have to keep a skeleton crew with me at all times, chief among them Jean Bethell, my executive secretary, who has been with me for years, and Sam Hicks, my right-hand man, who is a good mechanic, a skillful driver,

* William Morrow & Company, Inc.; 1965.

41

Dick DeShazer loves the water and loves boats.

a "bronc stomper," ranch owner, hunter, outfitter, tracker, camper, outdoor cook and, of late, has become a pretty darn good boatman. He has also written articles for various magazines as well as a book on herb remedies, *Desert Plants and People.**

The DeShazers usually accompany us on overnight trips.

Dick is a very busy individual. He has a force of highly trained salesmen under him. He has a stock of boats so he can

* The Naylor Company; 1966.

sell anyone anything that the prospective customer may want in marine transportation.

Dick has high-quality used boats which have had the initial depreciation taken off and which are good, honest values. He also has new boats representing the last word in comfort and refinements. He is an alert, aggressive businessman; but he sells boats because he loves the water and loves boats. And when an opportunity presents itself to go out for a night or two, or on an annual vacation of a week or two, Dick is there.

Sam Hicks.

A new house cruiser for Dick DeShazer's Yacht Center arrives on a flat car . . .

. . . a crew gets it ready for unloading . . .

*. . . then a specially designed vehicle straddles the track, lifts the
house cruiser off the flat car, and moves onto the highway.*

His wife, Moyne, is a competent assistant to Dick. She loves
to camp, is a talented painter and ceramist, is thoroughly
adjustable and accepts conditions as they arise—all without
"turning a hair," as the saying goes. She is also easy on the
eyes.

Jean Bethell and her two sisters, Peggy Downs and Ruth
(Honey) Moore, were secretaries in the law office when I was
practicing law in Ventura.

The three have been with me during all of my career as a
writer. They know the people I know. They know how to
handle any situation which may come up in the business.
They work long hours, obsessed with a determination to take
everything off my shoulders which they can possibly handle;
and they have made my career their life's work.

I could never repay the debt that I owe them.

Moyne DeShazer pretending she doesn't know that I am stealing a picture.

We traveled extensively in various countries before my television interests chained us pretty much to one place. We have encountered dangers, have been in tight situations where these women have had to use their heads when encountering antiforeign sentiment in native religious ceremonies in faraway lands.

Two of them were trapped with me in a secret Haitian voodoo ceremony where the crowd turned hostile, and only calm presence of mind saved our lives.

And always these secretaries have worked, pounding out words from the tips of busy fingers—millions on millions of words which have, in turn, been sold profitably in the fiction markets of the world.

CHAPTER THREE

The Delta Country

Since this book is going to concern itself with further explorations in the Delta country, let's take a rather comprehensive look at the places we're going to explore.

The Delta country is rich in history, and that history, in turn, affects the nature of the country itself.

Decades ago—before the days of gasoline engines, automobiles, paved highways, diesel-powered trucks, and all sorts of power machinery for lifting, stacking, grading, and storing —California agriculture was centered around the horse, the mule, the "Fresno" scraper, the Chinese coolie, and determined American ranchers.

There were heavy, powerful horses for pulling loads. There were thin-skinned, light-boned nervous horses for trotting along with the buggy. The roads were deep and rutted— dusty in summer, muddy in winter.

Water transportation was, therefore, a boon to the community, and the rivers were indeed busy places.

The rivers are still busy places; but recreation has largely supplanted the transportation of agricultural products— although such cities as Stockton and Sacramento are still supplied by oceangoing steamers which come through the

Golden Gate, cross San Francisco Bay, and then go up the deepwater channels which are maintained to each city.

In addition to all this, many products such as gasoline are delivered by barges, pushed by powerful tugs which go up the Sacramento River as far as Colusa.

Water from the Feather River has been largely used for agriculture, but there are parts of the river which can be used by shallow-draft boats and outboard motors.

Taken by and large, however, the main waterways are formed by the Sacramento River with its tributary sloughs, the North Fork of the Mokelumne, the South Fork of the Mokelumne, and the San Joaquin River with its tributary sloughs. All of these drain into the Delta region which, in turn, widens into the great reaches of San Francisco Bay.

Skirting the Delta region are wide superhighways along

Along the deep waterway, ships from all over the world are being loaded and unloaded.

Barges being loaded with sugar beets.

which diesel-powered trucks roar interminably in a never-ending procession.

Within the Delta region itself the roads, for the most part, run along the tops of the levees. These roads are winding, relatively narrow, but from them it is possible to get a good view of many of the waterways.

The cities of Sacramento and Stockton are the queen cities of the Delta. Sacramento, the state capital, is a thriving, sprawling city with politics, agriculture, and commerce vying for precedence.

Stockton is a delightful city of homes and stores, a deep-water port shipping thousands of tons, receiving goods from all over the world. It is at the head of a dredged channel and the big freighters gliding up the waterway sometimes seem to be mirages of huge ships in a dry field.

Modesto can also be classed as one of the Delta cities; and

49

Thousands of pleasure craft cruise the Delta.

Tracy, Antioch, Rio Vista, Walnut Grove, and Locke all play an important part in the economic life of the community.

For the most part, the waterways are still the dominant feature of the Delta and the thousands of pleasure craft represent the really big attraction, second only to the pulse of commerce as the big steamers slip silently by.

How different things are now from what they were fifty to seventy-five years ago when the automobile was virtually unheard of, when our so-called good roads were not even an engineering dream.

In those days, the farmer loaded his produce on a heavy wagon, hitched up a couple of powerful horses, and hauled the load to town.

The merchant who bought it transferred the load to a huge warehouse and waited until one of the big riverboats came swishing in to a landing.

At that time, sweating manpower transferred literally tons

and tons of deadweight to the boat and removed tons and tons of merchandise to be placed in the warehouse. Then the boat gave a blast from its deep-toned whistle, the paddle wheels revolved, and the boat was on its way to the next stop.

The river literally represented the economic lifeblood of the community.

Now, all is changed. The big river steamships are a thing of the past. Oceangoing freighters churn up the deepwater channels to Stockton and Sacramento, but the rivers and the sloughs would be almost deserted were it not for recreational boating.

The Delta King, *one of the last of the palatial riverboats.*

It is a painful experience to come across some of these majestic riverboats, which in their day were the last word in luxurious travel, tied up at docks or rotting away in the middle of an asparagus field.

The *Delta King*, however, is about to move into a brand-new career and it may be one that is in many ways as exciting as its former life.

My friend, Melvin Belli (the spectacular, controversial lawyer who was characterized by the *Saturday Evening Post* some years back as "The King of Torts"), and a partner, Max Mortenson, have, I understand, purchased the *Delta King* and intend to use it as a sort of floating hotel and dining emporium at some place down the river—probably off the Berkeley Aquatic Playground.

They have taken the heavy machinery out of the boat but have refurbished the rooms and brought out the finish of the

The main maritime thoroughfares are churned by thousands of propellers.

The Whit-Craft and Ken Craft.

wonderful old teakwood. They have put in chandeliers and, in general, have kept the spirit of the era of the riverboats.

Melvin Belli, who never does things by halves, is having one of the spacious staterooms fitted up as his own "Admiral's Room," and is looking forward to spending much of his time living aboard.

Belli's exuberant personality, his drive, his fertile imagination, and his love of California history guarantee that there are new days in store for the majestic *Delta King*.

Once again the sound of lighthearted laughter will float out across the moonlit waters; once again the rhythm of dance music will furnish a romantic background for the sheer enjoyment of life, which is youth incarnate.

And the older, more sedate people can bask in the luxury of a bygone era, living in the midst of palatial splendor, standing

53

A "camper" houseboat ready to be loaded on a pickup.

perhaps apart from the others on the deck, leaning against the teakwood rail, looking out over the waters and thinking of the days when the deep-throated whistle sounded from the foggy shores of the Stockton Channel, as the huge boat felt its way through the night and the fog on some of its more dangerous trips.

Getting a boat of this size up the river—particularly in the fog—was an accomplishment which called for phenomenal skill.

Those foggy nights were, however, interspersed with warm, moonlit nights when the throb of the engines and the swish of water furnished a soothing obligato for a memorable journey upriver.

On such nights the floating castle would glide up the channel, the epitome of gaiety and luxury. Under the magic touch of Melvin Belli and his partner, the boat bids fair to resume its place on the river.

As the saying goes, one door never closes but another opens.

54

Life on the river was at a low ebb as the trucks and the highways started furnishing the transportation connecting the ranchers directly with the centers of population. Then came the outboard motor—at first a racket-producing nuisance, which gradually has been refined into a smooth-running dependable mechanism.

New techniques in manufacturing of waterproof surfaces such as fiberglass and the synthetic resins, the development of trailers on which really good-sized boats can be carried behind automobiles—all brought the river back into its own, and now the main maritime thoroughfares are churned by thousands of propellers.

Some of these boats are remarkably ingenious in construc-

By putting down swivel pontoons, the camper becomes a miniature houseboat.

The more active younger crowd are enthusiastic about water skiing . . .

. . . and some become very expert indeed.

tion, such, for instance, as the "camper" which fits a pickup bed for camping on dry land, then, by putting down its pontoons, becomes a miniature houseboat.

The back stretches of the waterways are still relatively deserted, so the owner of a houseboat can leave the dock where he keeps his boat and, within a short time, have his boat tied up in placid waters against a levee, fishing for catfish, or can just stretch out, resting and relaxing.

The younger, more active crowd are enthusiastic about the sport of water skiing. Their boats are ever searching for open waters. The light, shallow-draft cruisers skim about on trips of exploration, gliding over the water at what would have been unheard-of speeds a few years ago. Seagoing cruisers find their way up the deeper channels, while good-sized sailboats have their regular harbors where the owners gather for recreation.

In recent years there has been a big boom in the boat business, particularly rental of houseboats.

These young ladies turned a sturdy houseboat into a comfortable floating apartment. Here they are flanked by the Author and Dick DeShazer.

Houseboats of varying styles, capable of sleeping relatively large numbers of people, can be rented by the day, week, or month.

Sometimes several families will rent two or three houseboats, which all proceed together and all tie up together at night.

When one compares the costs of taking a family on a vacation trip by automobile, stopping at motels, eating meals at restaurants, with the cost of a houseboat vacation where one can have camp cooking and where catfish and bass can furnish much of the protein food content, it is easy to see why houseboat rentals are becoming exceedingly popular.

These houseboats range from the catamaran type, which are powered by outboard motors, to the houseboat cruiser, which is a deluxe affair. The well-known feature writer, Walter Blum of the *San Francisco Examiner,* described my houseboat cruiser as a floating, high-class apartment.

These houseboat rental agencies vary all the way from the individual who has one houseboat, which he is willing to rent when it is not in personal use, to such places as Leisure

Rental houseboats at Leisure Landing.

Joyful vacationers in a rented houseboat ply the inland waterway.

Landing, which has some thirteen houseboats and cruisers of all kinds for rental.

During the season, Leisure Landing is a very busy place indeed. A group of vacationers who have finished their cruise will bring in a houseboat and move out their things. Within a matter of seconds, a trained crew takes over. Each person in this crew has a certain specific job. One checks the motor, sees that the oil is changed and the motor is properly tuned up. Another person washes the outside of the boat. Another person goes over the inside with a vacuum cleaner. The crew works rapidly and with perfect coordination.

Within a couple of hours that boat is ready to be taken out again, and usually a new group of people are standing by, prepared to stow away their things the minute they can go aboard.

Four happy vacationers . . .

When one realizes that each of these boats rents at from around fifty dollars a day up, it is evident that the monthly totals of such rentals can run into big money. And Leisure Landing is only one of several outfits engaged in rentals.

These boats which are rented out by Leisure Landing are equipped with citizen's band radios powerful enough to come in from just about any part of the Delta. If a renter has any trouble anywhere, all he needs to do is to pick up the citizen's band radio, call in to Leisure Landing, say, "I'm up in The Meadows. We hit a piece of driftwood with the propeller and bent one of the blades."

Leisure Landing will come right back, "Stay where you are.

We'll have a boat with a new prop up there within a couple of hours. Is there anything else you want?"

This is the sort of service which makes friends and builds business.

When I last checked with Leisure Landing it had seven Whit-Crafts, one River Queen, and five Trojan cruisers on its rental list. It was able to supply just about anything the customer wanted.

From the standpoint of the owner, getting from seven hundred and fifty to twelve hundred and fifty dollars for two weeks' rental for a house cruiser is a good thing. From the standpoint of the customer who wants a unique vacation where he needs only to drive a few hours over freeways, park his car, step aboard a houseboat and almost instantly be in a new world, the package is a delightful one. If two or perhaps three congenial couples want to pool their funds and spend their vacation together, there is an opportunity for rest, recreation, swimming, sunbathing, fishing, hilarious fun, and plenty of sleep—all at a cost that represents a real bargain.

. . . wait at the guest dock at Giusti's for supplies.

The interesting thing about a houseboat is that you don't have to go someplace to be on your vacation. The minute you step aboard the houseboat and cast loose the lines you are there. It isn't like an automobile vacation where a person has to drive three and four days in order to get to the place where he wants to spend his vacation, then drive three or four days getting back.

In the Delta country one can make rental reservations, leave from almost any part of California in the morning, and be sleeping that night on a houseboat tied up in some little cove away from all the noises of civilization, slumbering in the calm tranquillity of utter silence and sleeping as late as anyone wants the next morning.

I have recently made it a point to talk with people who have rented boats for their vacations and find them so enthusiastic that I feel convinced the rental business is going to be booming during the next few years.

One can cruise in secluded waters . . .

. . . and find peace and quiet.

One can cruise in secluded waters or he can get on the main channel. He can stock up with groceries and cook what he wants when he wants, or he can tie up at guest docks along the way, replenish his supplies and, if he wants, eat at some of those fabulous little restaurants which serve home cooking.

It's a good way to get fourteen full days of enjoyment out of a two weeks' vacation, to return rested and relaxed.

Houseboats are, for the most part, family affairs—as are the big cruisers; and the house cruiser combines the easy handling of the cruiser with the deluxe facilities of living on water, which are to be found only in the high-class houseboat.

These boats have just about every modern convenience— bearing in mind, of course, that since space is at such a pre-

The interesting thing about a houseboat is that you don't have to go some place to be on your vacation.

mium on the water, everything has to be designed with a maximum of efficiency.

Then there are many thousands of open boats powered with outboard motors. These outboard motors are now so efficient that the little runabouts can dart over the water like dragonflies.

Such boats can, of course, be used for fishing as well as for exploration and travel. They are relatively inexpensive, can be placed quickly and easily on trailers and transported behind automobiles over any necessary distance to the point of launching in the waterways.

The owner of one of these boats can leave his home in San Francisco early in the morning and an hour and a half later can be launching his craft at any one of the numerous launching ramps in the Delta region.

64

He can then cruise many carefree miles during the day, stopping at any one of many dozen resorts for gasoline and supplies, ice-cold beer, savory hamburgers or hot dogs. He can try his luck at fishing for striped bass, black bass, catfish, or blue gills. He can get back to the launching place before dark, put his boat back on the trailer, and drive home; or he can spread a sleeping bag and spend the night.

Fishing furnishes a great attraction, but simply exploring the inland waterways in a light, fast boat which fairly skims over the water is a great thrill.

There is quite a bit of life in the Delta waters during the week, but on weekends the people literally come pouring in. The ramps are busy launching one boat after another. The big cruisers ply the waters, the sailboats come up the deepwater channels from the bay region, the houseboat enthusiasts go out and tie up where there is good fishing, relax and rest, and the whole Delta country is throbbing with life.

The Delta makes an ideal vacation land for the cruising enthusiast.

On Friday, Saturday, and Sunday nights, literally thousands of people dine at the fine restaurants which are sprinkled throughout the Delta country from Antioch to Rio Vista.

These restaurants, many of them with modest exteriors, serve food which brings people back in droves again and again and again.

Then there are the places which can be reached both by car and boat, but which cater mostly to the cruising tourist whose appetite has become sharpened by the cool, fresh air of the waterways.

There are dozens of these places along the Delta waterways, places where the boats can be left at hospitable "guest docks" while the owners have coffee, sandwiches, or in many places a full-course dinner.

On Sundays the whole Delta country teems with life.

Sailboats come up the deepwater channels from the Bay region.

And some of these places—such as Giusti's—are so famous for good food that motorists drive for miles over the levee roads to have lunch or dinner, while many of the boatmen literally make the place their headquarters.

Giusti's was a famous restaurant and roadhouse during the days of the early mining rush—the golden days of California's pioneering history.

The place has descended in the family through the years, is still operated by the Giusti family, and still clings to the tradition of good home-cooked, appetizing fare at cheap prices.

The vegetables are grown in some of the most fertile soil in the world. The salads are garden crisp.

Seen from the rear, Giusti's shows the typical architecture of houses built along the levee.

Later on as we take our cameras and cast loose the lines on our house cruisers, we will be spending quite a bit of time at Giusti's. We will meet the various persons who really make the place what it is and keep up the tradition, so we will merely mention here in passing, so to speak, Manuel Morais, the "Mo" of the place; Lorenzo Giannetti, the "Lo" of Giusti's; Dolores Morais, Mo's wife; and Irene Giusti, Dolores' mother.

These people, incidentally, are some of the most wonderful, friendly people on the river, and Giusti's radiates their warm hospitality.

Or one can stop in at Korth's Pirates Lair for breakfast—where Jim Meuhlbauer and his wife, who formerly presided at The Beacon Resort, now have charge of the eating facilities —cruise in a leisurely manner up the channel, pause for a swim or a couple of hours' fishing, be at Giusti's for a superb noonday meal, and an hour or so later be anchored in The Meadows—considered by many to be the most beautiful part of the Delta country.

While they were at The Beacon, the Meuhlbauers established a reputation for breakfasts which made them known the length and breadth of the Delta country. Yachtsmen would make it a point to come miles to tie up and have their Saturday and Sunday morning breakfasts at The Beacon.

Korth's, by the way, is one of the most beautiful of all the marinas on the Delta. It has a spacious harbor with a great sweep of grassy lawn sloping down to the water, palm trees growing profusely—and, over all, an atmosphere of complete relaxation.

Korth, who owns the place, has a remarkable eye for scenic beauty; and his palatial residence, which is somewhat removed from the resort center, represents a unique architectural concept and the last word in gracious, luxurious living.

There are dozens of marina restaurants in the Delta country, each famous in its way for a particular type of food.

Wanda's Restaurant on Bethel Island is a well-known breakfast place with home cooking and fast service. Lunch and dinner are also served both at a counter and at booths. The place is well patronized both by fishermen and local business people.

The Bel-Isle Club, owned by my friend Irving Podris, has a representative menu but is justly famous for its rib eye steaks and Chinese food.

Alfred Wong, the Chinese cook, can turn out a complete dinner of several courses, combining the best in Chinese food—and can also cook rib eye steaks so juicy and flavorful that whenever I go there I wish I were twins so that I could order both the steak and the Chinese dinners.

Recently my friends, John Mart and Joe Silva, have opened a "chicken shack" on Bethel Island featuring high-grade

69

barbecue dishes. And, up the Stockton Channel, there is the beautiful Tiki Lagun, which we will visit later on.

The Riverview Restaurant in Antioch has picture windows looking out over the water. Parking space for automobiles is on a pier directly in front of the restaurant, and there is a long float at which boats can be moored so that diners can come to the restaurant by water.

This is on the Stockton deepwater channel, and quite frequently diners have the thrill of seeing a lighted freighter going up or down river—the ship, in the inland surroundings, seeming unbelievably huge. And, despite the fact it is moving at relatively slow speed because of the narrow channel, watching it glide past makes one realize the ease with which huge cargoes can be moved through the water from city to city, nation to nation.

There are many other restaurants in the Delta country which are comparable with good eating places anywhere.

I don't know why this is, except that probably the places

On Mondays, when Giusti's is closed, the guest dock is frequently deserted.

keep the same personnel year after year; and because competition is so keen, each restaurant vies with the other to maintain a high quality.

Or looking at it from another angle, these restaurants depend upon regular customers. The fishermen and yachtsmen come back week after week; word-of-mouth advertising brings in whatever new customers there are, so the restaurants make it a point to maintain quality. They have to.

In fact, the eating places in the Delta are such that they are worthy of a chapter in themselves.

In addition to the fishermen and the boating enthusiasts, people come from miles around just to enjoy the cooking.

And, of course, it is axiomatic that when one has a group of good restaurants to choose from, the eating standard is so high that poor competitors stand no chance at all. The net result is that *all* the restaurants in such a community are exceptional.

It is for that reason that we have certain cities which are known as good eating cities.

For instance, San Francisco is noted throughout the world as a good eating city. New Orleans is a good eating city. Boston and New York are good eating cities. And there are dozens of others—places where the general standards are so high that a mediocre competitor couldn't keep open.

There are also Mexican restaurants in the Delta country. Unfortunately, the tragedy of the *bracero* program has put some of these Mexican restaurants out of business.

These were not intended for the tourist trade. They are restaurants where the *braceros* can get quality Mexican food at reasonable prices. The menus feature the highly spiced, genuinely "hot" Mexican dishes which are so dear to the heart of the Mexican laborer, who is a mass of rawhided muscle capable of performing the highly specialized "stoop labor" in the fields.

When the *bracero* program was terminated, it represented an economic hardship to many vegetable growers, but it was a body blow to some of the little hole-in-the-wall restaurants where some skillful Mexican cook could make chili colorado, which no American could possibly hope to duplicate.

However, there are still several of these Mexican restaurants in operation. The furnishings are extremely plain, tablecloths are unknown, but the food is a gustatory delight to those who appreciate Mexican cooking.

Businessmen in the Delta have found these *bracero* restaurants, and it is possible to see well-dressed guests dining in these plainly furnished restaurants seated in close proximity to laborers who have spent a backbreaking day harvesting tomatoes and who are now relaxing with *tortillas, chiles rellenos,* and *cerveza.*

On weekends, cars come piling into the Delta country and business booms. The yachtsmen and the fishermen get set for a big weekend. The stores are nearly all open Saturday and Sunday. Many of the bait stores open at six in the morning; some serve coffee and doughnuts.

Bait is big business.

Tons of frozen sardines and fresh-water clams are sold to the hordes of eager fishermen. On Monday, the Delta habitues emerge from the avalanche of weekend business; and Tuesday is the day the Delta residents take to rest and relax.

CHAPTER FOUR

A Typical Cruise

My adventures in the Delta country during the summer of 1964 had been largely confined to the North Fork of the Mokelumne River and to the country to the east. I wanted to get a look at some of the country to the west.

Jean Bethell, Richard DeShazer, Sam Hicks, and I decided to take a trip in the River Queen house cruiser—starting from Richard's Yacht Center at the Bethel Island bridge, skirting Frank's Tract, passing Korth's Pirates Lair, going to the B & W Resort; then turning into Georgiana Slough, and from there into the Sacramento River just below Walnut Grove, and following the Sacramento River to Sacramento, and on up to Knights Landing.

For some years I had been a member of the Knights Landing Outboard Motor Club, and we had explored the river between Knights Landing and Colusa—a rather considerable distance when one takes into consideration the force of the current of the Sacramento River, which is something to be reckoned with.

However, I knew that the army engineers had been ordering trees removed from the slopes of the levees, and I wanted to see to what extent this had been carried out above Sacramento and what effect it had had on the levees themselves.

73

Jean Bethell and Moyne DeShazer gas up the Valco cruiser.

As I remembered it, some of these trees along the levee banks were eighty to a hundred feet in height. They were magnificent shade trees which made boating and tying up for a few hours an unmitigated pleasure.

In the places where the trees have been removed and rock faces put on the river side of the levees, the river becomes relatively uninteresting. One has to get his pleasure from the boating rather than from the scenery.

People with whom I have talked seem to feel that the levees are more permanent where the trees have been removed and rock faces placed on the sides. However, this is an ambitious undertaking and it is not going to be finished overnight or in the course of a year or two. I have also noticed that there are plenty of places where the trees have been removed from the levee and, before the levee has been faced with rock, the river has exerted an alarming toll of erosion.

I, personally, have a feeling that about the time the trees have all been removed, practical considerations will show that it would have been better to have left them where they were.

However, the Delta is fertile country. Trees seem to sprout everywhere. Vegetation even grows from the tops of old pilings which have been placed in the channel. I intend to be philosophical and rejoice at what we have left while we have it—the remaining shade trees and the leisure and freedom to enjoy them. There are places where the trees continue to remain in place, and there is always the charm of boating on the water.

It is difficult to analyze this charm.

I remember many, many years ago when I felt the same way about an automobile. It was a pleasure to get behind the wheel of a good car and drive leisurely along the highway, noticing the scenery and experiencing the exhilarating sense of motion.

A huge dredge which has just come through the drawbridge at Giusti's and is now working its way up the river.

These automobiles and the roads on which they were operated would get you there and get you back; but the pleasure of driving and watching the scenery was such that, on a free afternoon, one could go for a drive just for the sheer pleasure of driving.

Then the public demand for speed and ever more speed made for faster cars, wider roads, and shorter driving time when the road was clear.

The net result is that nowadays, on a free afternoon, one can travel much farther in a much faster car but at a much slower pace than one wants to go, hampered by the numbers of other cars and whipped by occupational impatience. Saturday- and Sunday-afternoon driving is no longer any pleasure at all.

Boating now gives me the same pleasure I got from driving years ago. I like to glide over the water, the breeze in my face; I like the freedom from restraint, the sense of motion.

Vegetation growing from the tops of piles which have been pounded into the slough.

Boating now gives me the same pleasure I used to get from driving years ago.

I get this same feeling boating on the river, no matter what type of boat I am using. All I want is a *good* boat.

There is this feeling of independence, of being a part of nature; and, of course, the feeling of motion has always appealed to man. There is, moreover, a sense of freedom from the cares and worries which tend to surround the individual when he is part of a human ant colony struggling in endless turmoil in what, at times, seems to be a hopeless treadmill.

There is also the marvelous feeling which is inherent in the anticipation experienced in getting ready for a boating trip.

Sam and I started storing ice, clothing, and provisions, preparatory to this Knights Landing trip. Jean went to the market and planned the menus. Dick DeShazer struggled manfully with a whole series of last minute-problems so that he could get away at the earliest possible moment.

The River Queen explores the Mokelumne River.

As I have said earlier, the River Queen is a floating deluxe apartment. It has a steel, watertight hull with hatches which open up to disclose huge storage spaces—and we took full advantage of all this storage space.

The cruiser has an electric refrigerator with a freezing compartment, but since we had lots of plastic containers which would keep ice for a long time and loads of room, we loaded aboard extra supplies of ice for chilling watermelons, a varied assortment of cold drinks, and keeping fresh vegetables.

The day was hot, but the steel body of the River Queen resting on cool water made the interior so comfortable that we didn't even bother to turn on the air-conditioning unit.

The boat was in one of Bud Remsburg's covered berths, the

light was dim, the shade was cool, and Sam and I loaded our gear—Sam doing the heavy work while I carried cameras, films, and lighter stuff.

Sam is a good-natured giant—tall and strong, with long legs, big wrists and hands, and an unlimited capacity for responsibility and achievement.

As I get older, it is a pleasure to let these younger men take over.

Dick DeShazer is a real yachtsman. When he came aboard he carried his extra clothes, shaving kit, and the things he needed in a briefcase.

Yachtsmen and aviators are certainly accustomed to traveling light.

Personally, I travel heavy.

When I would take pack trips on hunting expeditions into the wild mountainous country I always told the outfitter, "You've got packhorses; I've got money. Put an extra packhorse in the string."

I will admit that at times I carried a weird assortment of articles.

For instance, I noticed that the "dudes," who had previously ridden the horses I was destined to ride later, would let the bridle reins drag when they stopped and got off. The heavy-footed trail horses would step on a rein and break it off, whereupon the wrangler would "splice" the rein.

As the next dude in line, I would have bridle reins that were spliced in one or two places.

This can be exceedingly annoying. The average dude horse wants loose reins. He is in a string of horses on a narrow mountain trail. He knows where he is going. He knows the other horses. He knows the trail. He knows the wrangler. He knows exactly where they are going to camp that night, and he has a pretty good idea of how long it is going to take to get to that camp. If he is a good, conscientious horse, he is going to keep his place in the string.

He doesn't want the dude to *ride* him, he wants to *carry* the dude.

Therefore, at regular intervals, the horse will bite down on the bit, give his powerful neck a surge, and jerk the reins through the fingers of the surprised dude.

If the bridle reins are spliced, when the splice comes ripping through the fingers of the dude's hand, it can give him an uncomfortable sensation.

Therefore, I always made it a point to carry my own bridle reins.

I remember on one trip in the primitive area of Idaho when the famous Bill Sullivan and his brother-in-law, Ted Williams, were piloting us, a wrangler from a nearby outfit came riding into our camp one night to pass the time with Ted Williams, whom he knew quite well.

The wrangler took a look at our outfit and particularly at my duffel bags. He wanted to know how in hell any dude could fill up all those duffel bags with material which by any stretch of the imagination could be considered necessary or useful on a trip of that kind.

I held my peace because there was nothing else for me to do.

It happened, however, that this wrangler had tied his horse to a tree by the bridle reins. He sat visiting with us until quite late and then, in the darkness as he approached the horse, his cowboy boot caught in a root and the wrangler stumbled. He instinctively threw out his hands to catch himself, his horse snorted, jerked back, and broke both bridle reins about six inches from the bit.

That wrangler had a picturesque vocabulary. The thought of trying to splice bridle reins and riding over trails in the darkness made him use purple language and lots of it.

Spliced reins might be all right for a dude, but you never see a wrangler riding with spliced reins.

So I got up, walked over to one of my duffel bags, reached

in, took out a new pair of bridle reins, quietly walked over to where the wrangler was standing, and handed him the brand-new pair of expensive bridle reins.

"Just take these," I said.

He looked at me with wide-eyed amazement. "Where in hell did you get these reins?" he asked.

"Out of my duffel bag," I told him casually. "You see, I'm a veteran camper, and every once in a while some damn fool wrangler will tie up a horse by the bridle reins, then 'spook' the horse and break the reins. I always go prepared to help out at such a time.

"You'll find these reins are very strong and hard to break."

I turned and walked away.

The guy was so grateful for the reins he was willing to take a little ribbing, yet he wasn't *entirely* certain he was being ribbed.

My talk had the effect of paralyzing his vocal cords.

Ted Williams came out to help him. They put on the new bridle reins and the wrangler rode away.

The next year when I was in that country, Bill Sullivan tipped me off. "Don't let that wrangler know you're here," he said, "or he'll take a shot at you."

"How come?" I asked.

"The damn fool went into a bar in Challis and told the story," Bill Sullivan said. "Prior to that time, he had always been considered an honest man, but the story of a dude taking a pair of bridle reins out of a duffel bag for a wrangler who had tied up his horse by the bridle reins and then spooked him was too much for the people in the bar to take.

"They promptly branded the guy the biggest and most imaginative liar in the Middle Fork. Just keep away from him."

I kept away from him.

But I still maintain the habit of traveling heavy. However, the River Queen is built to take it and, after all, a couple of extra duffel bags only means one more trip up and down the ramp—for Sam.

Sam had the motors warmed up by the time Dick got everything settled, and we were off.

The River Queen, powered with twin Ford Interceptors with an inboard-outboard drive and cruiser bow, is capable of maintaining a very satisfactory cruising speed—yet the interior is such that one moves about at will from main cabin to dining room, galley, bedroom, and "head" without constantly ducking and twisting.

It is made to sleep six comfortably, but it has ample space to carry sleeping bags, and decks which enable people to camp out—so that in clear weather quite a crowd can be accommodated.

The four of us on the River Queen were surrounded with lots of room.

Courteous yachtsmen go no faster than five miles an hour when cruising past docks which line the shores of the slough. In this way, the wake is not sufficiently violent to rock the boats at the mooring; and, in leaving our mooring, we had about fifteen minutes of five-mile-an-hour progress in Dutch Slough before we got in the clear.

Then we turned into Sand Mound Slough and began to open up the engines.

We were in no screaming hurry. We kept the engines from two-thousand to twenty-five hundred revolutions, although we could have gone up above thirty-five hundred to four thousand had we so desired.

However, we were as cozy as though we had been visiting in an apartment. Sitting there in the living-room cabin of the River Queen, we relaxed in comfortable chairs or on a padded davenport and stretched our legs, knowing that we weren't going to have any interruptions. No problems, no stress, no strain.

It is a wonderful feeling!

Kenneth Brown, the champion skier, illustrates a difficult maneuver on a single ski.

We glided along Sand Mound Slough to the border of Frank's Tract.

Frank's Tract needs a little explaining. It was at one time a huge ranch, but, like all the Delta country ranches, the agricultural ground was below the water level. The levees kept out the water.

Then, one night, something happened. The levee broke, the water came pouring in and, as a result, what was once one of the most prosperous ranches in the community is now an enormous lake some five miles across.

The owners of the land, claiming that the government had taken over the responsibility of maintaining the levees, insisted that the government "get its water out of here." The government couldn't find any way of getting the water out of there. There was too much of it.

Walnut Grove and the companion city of Locke have the early Chinese type architecture . . .

So now a part of the property has been taken for a state park and there is a huge shallow lake of water, which is something of a landmark in the Delta region. Rumor has it that there is an orchard with the tree limbs just a few feet, and in places only a few inches, below the surface. Fishermen may get their lines snapped on a submerged tractor or a piece of expensive farm machinery.

Personally, I have never been anxious to find out, and most of the conservative boaters feel the same way. They skirt around the outside of Frank's Tract—back of the line of the old levee until they come to the Old River; then to the San Joaquin River, cross the Stockton deepwater channel, pass Korth's Pirates Lair; and then go up the Mokelumne River past a whole series of interesting marinas and resorts.

84

Someday I hope to have the time to explore some of these resorts and clubs. Later on, we will take a look at Perry's—a short distance above the Pirates Lair.

We were familiar with the Beacon Resort when Meuhlbauers had it, but I haven't been there recently; and I have yet to explore some of the other interesting marinas and restaurants which dot the west bank of the river. (The resorts are on the west bank because it is possible to reach them via a good road.)

So we went on to the B & W Resort, a beautiful place which I hope to explore on another trip—but today it was simply a junction point where we turned to the west, left the Mokelumne River, and entered Georgiana Slough.

We followed the leisurely windings of Georgiana Slough up to the drawbridge, then into the Sacramento River and up to Walnut Grove and—just above Walnut Grove—the city of Locke, which is really worth a chapter in itself.

At Locke there is one of the old warehouses, hundreds

. . . which is a holdover from the early days of California.

of feet long, built out at the level of the levee with piles supporting the building out over the river.

In the old days, boat after boat landed at this warehouse to take on passengers and produce.

The warehouse was designed so that wagons could drive from the road along the levee right into the warehouse and unload. Then, when riverboats came, a chute could be rigged down to the loading deck and the produce slid down by gravity.

This was a conventional, easy method of loading these boats. Passengers could step out from the buildings at levee level, which put them on the upper passenger decks of the boats. The produce could be slid down by chute to the frieght decks, where stevedores would be engaged in stowing it away.

The whole loading operation gave employment to a large number of men, and the river was a very busy maritime thoroughfare.

Whenever I see one of these loading arrangements, I think of a story told me by my old friend, Captain Madden, who always chuckled over the story of "Hog" Riley.

It seems that Captain Riley had a little boat which was operating up the coast, picking up supplies here and there and running them in to San Francisco.

The boat, as Madden described it, was one with a little peanut-power motor which had a regular run carrying hides, produce, etc., in to San Francisco. Captain Riley—who was later to become known as "Hog" Riley—was a man of rather generous beam, and he was engaged in shipping hogs to San Francisco from a point down the coast.

The hogs were being loaded with a chute. That is, the fore-feet and hind feet were tied together; the hog was lifted onto the chute and turned loose. The force of gravity would carry the hog sliding down the smoothly polished chute into the hold; and the man in the hold would call out, "A hog, one—a hog, two—a hog, three—a hog, four"—and then at the fifth, he would call out, "A hog, tally."

In that way the shipment could be checked against the bill of lading.

It happened that after the fourth hog had gone down the chute, Captain Riley—heaving and tugging at a huge hog—somehow managed to get the hind legs of the animal untied, or the animal kicked his legs out of the knot.

The hog didn't want to go down that chute and didn't intend to go down. Captain Riley found himself caught off balance and suddenly realized he was catapulting down the chute.

The man in the hold—seeing a huge black body cascading down the chute—duly made a tally, raised his voice and reported to those above, "A hog, tally."

From that day on, Riley was known throughout the trade as "Hog" Riley.

Captain Madden also tells another story of "Hog" Riley. It seems Riley was casting off from one of the smaller ports at night. He was loaded with every bit of cargo he dared put on his little ship, and had huge bales of hides piled along the afterdeck obstructing the view of the helmsman to the rear. But Riley had lookouts out front and, since he was a veteran who sailed by compass course and made many of his runs at night, he didn't care about visibility. It was late at night when he finally gave the signal to cast off and started the motor, easing out into Stygian darkness.

The men stood watches; the Captain stood by the helmsman, giving him directions on times and compass. And then, about the time Captain Riley thought he should be picking up his familiar landmarks off San Francisco, a deep fog came in.

The Captain sounded the foghorn and, almost immediately, had an echo hurled back at him.

The use of an echo is, of course, one of the standard means

87

of navigating in a fog. The whistle is blown, the time is taken for the echo to return to the ship; the time is multiplied by the speed of sound, divided by two—and that is the distance the ship is offshore.

The promptitude with which the echo came blasting back at Captain Riley caused him the greatest consternation. He was within a few hundred feet of shore, somewhere at a place where he had no business having land anywhere around him.

Again the whistle sounded, and again the echo came blasting back.

Riley tried changing course and easing offshore, but he couldn't get offshore. The shore seemed to follow him. Wherever he went, he seemed to keep just a certain distance from the shoreline.

It wasn't until the first streaks of daylight blew away the few streamers of fog that Captain Riley realized someone had neglected to turn loose the stern line, and the boat had been pulling against the mooring of the wharf all night—changing courses, but never getting anywhere.

The story may be apocryphal; but Captain Madden vouched for its truth and used to tell it from time to time with the greatest glee.

It would, of course, take a certain combination of events to bring about such a happening, but Captain Madden was a veracious individual who insisted it was true. He was a hard-bitten salt who had had a variety of experiences throughout the world and could hold an audience fascinated telling stories of the Seven Seas.

To return to our trip, our house cruiser went on past the warehouse at Locke, the mysterious town that still has so much of the Oriental atmosphere. One almost feels he is in a provincial village in China when he starts wandering around the narrow side streets, down below the level of the levees.

There is a wonderful Chinese market here operated by my friends, the Kings, with a meat department under the guidance of George Marr. And there are several other markets in the place where one can obtain all sorts of Chinese delicacies.

There are, of course, logical reasons why the Chinese settled in Locke.

Many years ago, California was literally swarming with Chinese. The Chinese coolie did the heavy work in the hot sun for wages so small that one wondered he could live at all.

But the frugal Chinese lived, saved money, sent it back to China; and many of them returned to China relatively wealthy men. Chinese merchants opened stores, became shrewd buyers, selling their wares at a low margin of profit, and soon infiltrated the economy of the country.

When I was a young lad living at Oroville, the Chinese situation was as hot an issue as is the *bracero* program today.

Newspapers of the period talked of "the yellow peril."

The Chinese were a minority group suffering indignities which one can hardly realize.

Many kids considered it smart to throw rocks at a "Chinaman" whenever they saw him. There is, I believe, a decision in one of the old justice's courts that killing a "Chinaman" was no crime because murder consisted of killing a human being, and a Chinese was not a human being.

Be that as it may, the Chinese had no rights, no status. They worked for a pittance; they did work that the American laborer wouldn't consider; they saved their money; they became prosperous; and, eventually, they won the respect of the citizens everywhere.

Today, the Chinese—what few of them can be found in the country—are consummate merchandisers. They are shrewd buyers who recognize quality and operate on a small margin of profit.

The market operated by the Kings at Locke is a shining example.

George Marr has some of the choicest meat one can find anywhere, regardless of the size of the city or the market. The merchandise in the market is high quality and is well displayed, the prices are reasonable; and there are all sorts of Chinese delicacies—canned fresh lichee nuts, dried bean noodles, Chinese oyster sauce, and the pickled scallions which the chinese call *"sohn kayeu tau"*—but which are now being produced in quantity by the Japanese.

There is also the Chinese bean cake cheese, made out of bean curds which presumably are fermented in some way and then preserved. The squares of this Chinese cheese have an absolutely indescribable flavor—as pungent as horseradish, as rich as Camembert, as strong as Limburger.

I will admit that some of these Chinese delicacies require a little period of acquaintanceship before the palate develops a full-flavored friendship, but I love the Chinese food.

Years ago, I lived in China with a Chinese family. There wasn't a knife, fork, or silver spoon in the house, as far as tableware is concerned. We ate with chopsticks and porcelain china spoons. Naturally, I became quite adept with chopsticks, and think back with nostalgic memories of the times when the family sat around the table—each with his individual bowl of rice, but all of the other dishes in the center of the table. Each individual reached in with his chopsticks, picked out what he wanted, put it on his bowl of rice, ate a layer of rice, then returned to the central dishes for more of the food.

Those were in the days of long ago, as far as the Orient is concerned. At that time, the Chinese had the greatest respect for the Americans as a race.

I think back on those days and contrast them with what is happening today.

Now, the average Mainland Chinese hates our guts.

This has been brought about because we didn't like the

George Marr, Stanford King, and "Connie" King in the well-appointed market at Locke.

communist leadership of the Chinese and so, in order to punish the Chinese for going communist, we harassed them economically and politically in every way we could.

The inevitable result, of course, was that we managed to alienate the Chinese people and thereby made the communist rulers that much more secure in their jobs.

I sometimes wonder what would have happened if we had simply tried to keep the friendship and respect of the Chinese individual.

Perhaps the communist leaders would have been able to have turned the citizens against us anyway, but it would have been more of a job than if we ourselves hadn't helped do it.

I suppose I am unspeakably naive in international affairs, but I like people. I like to travel in foreign lands. I like to study foreign customs and try to appreciate types of thought which are not based on American patterns.

Salmon trollers.

More and more in my travels, I have found a creeping atmosphere of hostility and a spirit of "Yankee, go home!"

I suppose this decreasing prestige has been the inevitable result of necessary foreign policies, but sometimes I wonder.

I particularly wonder about Mainland China—where my former friends have now quit writing to me, but where thirty-odd years ago the American was universally respected.

But all this is a long way from the Delta country.

Anyhow, on this trip to Knights Landing we decided to pass up Walnut Grove and Locke, and kept moving smoothly on up the Sacramento River.

It was getting along in the afternoon when we passed Walnut Grove, but we didn't have to bother about the hour.

That is part of the charm of houseboating.

We had our beds along; we had our electric plant and electric lights; we had radio, television, air conditioning if we wanted it; and we had an abundance of food.

We were as much at home as the Canadian goose which had decided to spend the summer in the Delta country, and which went swimming majestically by.

So we kept on up the river until it began to get dark. Then we pulled in to the bank, tied up to a couple of trees, broke out the portable barbecue outfit, used the electric generator to fire up some charcoal, spread thick steaks on the broiler, brought out ice-cold beer, sourdough French bread which we toasted and buttered, had a crisp salad, and sat there in our little private domicile as completely isolated as though we had been on the ocean a thousand miles from shore—yet along the roads on the riverbank, there was a fairly steady stream of automobile traffic.

Those steaks were juicy, thick, and tender. They came from

A Canadian goose, summering in the Delta country, swims majestically by our house cruiser.

another market where we have always been able to get positively superb meat.

I think this is so largely true of the Delta country because the markets cater to boatmen who want barbecues and, therefore, demand the best.

I know that the markets at Bethel Island have some of the best meat I have ever been able to buy; and like so many other boatmen, we make it a point to obtain the very best which money *can* buy.

Sitting around the table on our house cruiser, dining leisurely and in an unhurried atmosphere, with tender juicy steaks two and a half inches thick and barbecued to perfection, the cares of the world certainly seemed far away.

The hot-water tank of the River Queen gave us an abundant supply of scalding hot water. The dishes presented almost no problem and, shortly after dinner, we turned out the lights and sat there in the warm darkness listening to the purling waters of the river, watching the occasional lights of passing automobiles on the riverbank.

Soon the tempo of conversation slowed; we became drowsy and went to bed.

I know that I had a night of deep, untroubled sleep—waking once or twice long enough to roll over, listening to the gurgling of waters as they swept past the steel hull. Tied to overhanging tree limbs some eight or ten feet offshore, we were completely isolated, thoroughly relaxed.

CHAPTER FIVE

Of Tender Steaks And Sharp Knives

We had decided we wanted an early start because today we would be bucking the current on the river. So Jean had "loaded" the coffee percolator before she went to bed.

In the morning, all she had to do was to press a button and within a few minutes the delightful aroma of coffee permeated the sleeping quarters.

I am not much of a coffee drinker and seldom touch it except on these houseboat trips, then I usually start with morning coffee. There is something about the aroma of the freshly made coffee mingling with the tang of fresh air along the water which makes an irresistible combination.

Each one busied himself with chores—making beds, getting the motors started, the moorings loose. And then we were under way just as the sun, coming from behind low clouds in the east, turned the water into gold.

We cooked breakfast while we were under way and ate while watching the shores slip by.

We were at Sacramento at about the time of the morning rush hour and, as we glided under the big bridges, we watched the automobiles rolling across overhead almost bumper to bumper and thought how fortunate we were.

We stopped at one of the marinas for gasoline and more

Returning to the River Queen, moored at the guest dock at Knights Landing, after lunch in town.

water, then went on up the river, coming to an exclusive residential district where beautiful mansions with sumptuous velvety lawns, huge shade trees, spacious grounds stretched to the tops of the levees.

These were truly beautiful houses and the estates were a pleasure to behold—looking like fine parks bordering the river.

We were getting into an area now where we found more and more trees. In places, the levees had been denuded and, in some places, surfaced with rocks. On the other hand, there were many places where apparently the natural growth had not been touched, and the trees towered high above the water, giving beautiful reflections and deep shade.

Shortly after noon, we reached Knights Landing, gassed the boat, and walked a few blocks into town where we found one of the modern roadside restaurants featuring hamburgers, hot dogs, and milk shakes.

We had lunch sitting in the shade, then returned to the boat.

It was getting hot now, and the breeze made by the motion of the boat was welcome as we went up the river.

The current was strong and very noticeable. Whenever a snag stuck up out of the water, the current swirled by it with waves and eddies; and we could tell from our progress that we were being slowed down materially.

I understand that the gasoline barge, pushed by a tugboat, makes it up the river from Sacramento to Colusa in eighteen hours but only takes six hours to come down. The distance, I believe, is around eighty miles, but the barge being loaded going up and empty coming down would also make a difference.

When I was a kid sixteen years old, I would have tackled a

Placid waters reflect trees along the riverbank.

problem of this sort with gusto and, within a matter of seconds, determined exactly how fast the current was running.

At the moment, the problem was too complicated; when I was a kid, it would have been too simple.

As I remember it, the problems they used to give us went something like this: Upon being asked how old he was, the man said, "If I were twice as old plus ten years, one-half of my age would be twenty-five years and two months." Question: How old was the man?

These were the types of problems I used to eat up; but as I grew older, if I had asked a man how old he was and he had given me any such a reply, I would have found better ways of occupying my time than by figuring "x plus 25, multiplied by 2."

Jean, Sam Hicks, and I had boated extensively from Knights Landing on north to Colusa. This was at a time some ten years ago when we had boats with outboard motors and were members of the Knights Landing Outboard Motor Club; so we didn't care particularly about going too far north of Knights Landing.

However, the day was yet young, so we went on up the river bucking the current until we'd reached a point seven or eight miles north of Knights Landing and then decided that we would have more fun turning around and exploring some of the Sacramento River country to the south rather than bucking the current for another thirty or thirty-five miles.

We had been warned by people who had made the trip by houseboat that north of Grimes, which was some twenty miles north of Knights Landing and up in the district of flooded rice fields, the mosquitoes were very bad indeed and virtually immune to the protective sprays designed to keep winged insects from their prey.

We rather wanted to find out for ourselves and had brought along a lot of insect repellent, but it had been a perfect trip and we hadn't even seen a mosquito. However, since both Sam and Dick like to sleep out on deck in their sleeping bags, we decided to let this part of our explorations wait for a later trip. So we turned the River Queen around and started moving rapidly downstream.

We passed Knights Landing and went on down to the place where the Feather River joins the Sacramento.

The Feather River is navigable for only short distances in various places.

Small boats can be trailer-launched above the check dam below Oroville—or at least they could some time ago—and here there are two or three miles of tree-lined waterways, the trees rich with mistletoe.

The water from the Feather River where it joins the Sacramento is clear and sparkling, and quite a number of boats were anchored near the mouth of the river.

We thought of stopping and exploring, but we had other places we wanted to see, and by that time it was getting along in the afternoon.

Great clumps of wild mistletoe cling to the trees which line the bank in places along the sloughs.

So we kept on going, retracing our steps until it got too dark to navigate with safety—when we found ourselves by chance in exactly the same place where we had spent the previous night.

Knowing of the location, the overhanging limb for the bow and the dead snag which would give us protection at the stern, we again tied up at our old mooring place, shut off the motors, and turned on the lights in the houseboat.

Instantly, we ceased to be travelers and became deluxe campers.

Sam got out the portable barbecue outfit, set it up on the bow, put in charcoal, and used the electric fire kindler to get the charcoal going.

Because the River Queen's hull is of heavy steel, it is possible for a portable barbecue grate requiring charcoal to be used with safety—just so the broiler has legs that are long enough for the heat from the bottom of the broiler not to descend onto the deck in too great a quantity.

Sailboats, graceful as gulls.

Because the River Queen's hull is heavy steel, it is possible to use a barbecue grate on the deck.

And because the bow structure is roomy, it is possible to get four or five director's chairs comfortably arranged around the barbecue grate.

We weren't in too great a hurry with those steaks because we had the entire evening at our disposal; and we sat there watching the lights of the cars rolling along the road topping the levee on the opposite side of the river, swapping memories of trips that we had taken and building air castles of trips that we wanted to take.

Because Dick DeShazer has been with us on many of our trips of desert exploration and has shared many adventures, we all had a lot to talk about.

In the meantime, Sam would from time to time turn the steaks, keeping the elevation of the grate above the coals at just the right distance so the steaks would be evenly done all the way through.

Personally, I dislike steaks which are seared on the outside, well-done for a quarter of an inch, medium-rare for a quarter of an inch, and cold in the center. I want my steaks to be done uniformly all the way through, and I want them a little on the rare side of medium-rare. At the same time, I like to have the juice literally spurt out when a *sharp* knife is used to cut the steak. And, regardless of what Emily Post may say, that red steak juice, delightfully warm, makes a wonderful liquid in which to dunk hot sourdough French bread which has been lightly toasted over the barbecue coals or perhaps heated in aluminum foil in an oven.

And because I have to watch my weight and everything I eat seems to have a knack of turning into fat, I have to rely on the joys of anticipation even more than the joys of realization.

So we sat there and watched the steaks cooking, swapped reminiscences, and were bathed in the velvety darkness of the warm night.

Then the steaks were ready along with the toast, and we adjourned to the dining room where we ate in a leisurely fashion—this time with some red table wine to keep company with the hot buttered French bread. The menu was, of course, the same as that of the night before; but when one has achieved perfection, why try to improve on it?

Our steak knives were razor-sharp. When I am eating steak, I want to use a *sharp* knife. And this does not mean the ordinary steak knife.

Most steak knives are kept in a special drawer. They are put around the plates when meat is served; and then they are gathered up by the dishwasher, put in a dishpan, and washed so that the edge of one knife rubs against the blade of another knife until, after half a dozen washings, the keen edges have completely disappeared—although if the knives are hollow ground they still do a fair job of steak cutting, if only a fair job.

102

But once one has tasted steak which has been cut with a really razor-sharp knife so that the fibers aren't compressed and the juice squeezed out by the pressure necessary to make the cut, I think he will have become a confirmed addict to the razor-sharp theory.

Of course, you can't do this around the house. A man can carry a belt knife which is so sharp that it is only necessary to rest it on top of the steak and draw it lightly across the meat in order to have a perfectly clean cut. Then when he is finished, he has only to polish that knife carefully under a stream of hot water, dry it, and then put it back in its sheath.

A knife which is kept in a drawer is seldom sharp. And any collection of knives which is washed in toto represents a household crime.

The average sheath knife is more or less of an ornament. But there are a few really good knives.

My friend, the late C. H. Dykeman, head of the Ford Publications, sent me a sheath knife which is made back in his neck of the woods by the Lee Olsen family, who have gone in for making hunting knives and nothing else.

These are relatively expensive and of top grade.

There is a concern up in Canada which makes the Russel hunting knife, which is very exceptional and which is, I believe, more moderately priced. There is also a hunting knife, I understand, made in Florida by Randall which is considered exceptional.

Lately, I have been carrying a "Buck" knife, which is quite a piece of cutlery.

I went through the factory in San Diego that makes them because I wanted to verify a story which I had heard to the effect that, after one of their knives is ready for the finishing touches and before it is allowed to go out of the factory, it must be able to cut a regular ¼-inch iron rivet without nicking the edge of the knife.

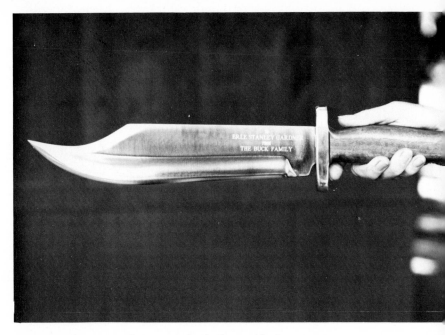

The Bucks presented one of their Bowie knives to me.

I couldn't believe this when I heard it, so I made a point of looking up the factory to find out.

It is true.

Before any knife leaves the place, they give it this acid test. They put the edge on a bolt, take a hammer and pound a deep cut into the bolt, then they inspect the edge of the knife. If the edge has been damaged in any way, the knife is discarded. If the edge remains truly sharp, free from any nick or blemish, the knife is finished up and sent out.

With steel that is this hard, it takes a little patience to keep a really razor-keen edge on the knife, but after it is once done, the knife holds the edge for a long time.

At the San Diego factory, I found the Buck family had been doing a lot of research on the famous "Bowie" knife, getting its true dimensions, weight, length, and balance.

The Author with his prized Bowie knife.

At long last they had been able to duplicate this famous knife and had made up a few. They were not for sale and were made only because the Bucks love knives and the Bowie knife had had such an effect on the Wild West when the West really was wild.

Some time later, the Bucks made me one of these duplicates of the Bowie knife and presented it to me.

It is one of my most prized possessions and is a truly remarkable souvenir. Bowie must have been an almost invincible antagonist when armed with such a knife.

Most veteran outdoor men are inordinately proud of their knives and take good care of them. I know quite a few people who have made a habit of honing their sheath knives while sitting around the campfire at night.

This much I do know—one who has never eaten a thick steak except by using the conventional steak knife is in for a pleasant surprise if he takes a razor-sharp sheath knife, so sharp that virtually no pressure is required, and cuts the steak with it.

Of course, in a restaurant where knives have to be handled wholesale, the knife with the serrated edge does a fairly good job, but it is a miniature saw rather than a knife. However, *nothing* can equal a good steak that is cut with a razor-keen knife; and experience has indicated to me that very, very few people have ever enjoyed the experience.

We ate the meal, of course, in the dining room of the boat surrounded by all the conveniences and luxuries of a small apartment.

It would have been nice to have sat out on deck for a while, but after our meal we found we were getting drowsy and some fifteen minutes spent out in the velvety darkness was all we could take before we started yawning, and it was still relatively early when we descended into the deep oblivion which comes from resting in the open.

106

CHAPTER SIX

Interesting Delta Dwellers

Steamboat Slough is one of the famous beauty spots of the Sacramento River. Actually, the slough is something of a short cut on the west side of the river and is used by many small boats. But, for the most part, it is known as an anchorage for boats that come up from San Francisco or from the west side of the inland waterway.

There are spots here where the trees have not been cut down. At such places there is good afternoon shade and there are a few sandy banks where there is good river swimming.

Yachtsmen are a gregarious type. Many dyed-in-the-wool yachtsmen get to know other yachtsmen, their boats, their idiosyncrasies; and when these people come to a good place to tie up they will tie their boats solidly together.

This seems to happen in "The Meadows" to the north of Giusti's, which is on the North Fork of the Mokelumne River, as well as in Steamboat Slough.

Particularly on holidays or long weekends during the yachting season there will be almost a solid string of boats.

I have said that many yachtsmen are gregarious. This is paradoxical in that many a yachtsman has bought his boat to get away from people.

However, this means that the yachtsman wants to get away from a certain class of people, from certain responsibilities, from a certain cross-section of his life. Once out on the water, there is a camaraderie which causes yachtsmen to cluster in groups under the spell of the outdoors as iron filings cluster around the poles of a magnet.

I presume that many of these people are personal friends—either members of the same yacht club or people who have known each other from other yachting trips—because I cannot imagine the pleasure of living cheek-by-jowl with a total stranger. But this much I do know—in all of these choice anchorages, one will find several yachts either tied solidly together or moored in such close proximity that one is all but touching the other.

Because we had gone to bed early and because we like to watch the early light on the water, we were early risers on this particular morning and I am afraid we went through the upper end of Steamboat Slough at too early an hour, despite the fact the sun was well up.

Most of the yachtsmen were still sleeping—or, rather, they were lying in that deliciously quiescent state where they were still in bed but were "thinking about" getting up.

As they heard our house cruiser go by, they raised their heads to look. And since there were quite a few boats tied up, we had quite an assortment of early-morning views—of tousled heads emerging from sleeping bags on deck, popping up to look through the cabin windows, and occasionally figures in pajamas looking out of open doors.

We were running at a very slow speed so as to make as little noise as possible and leave as small a wake as possible; but, since this was the magic time of day when people on vacation were taking a leisurely half hour to feel that they *should* get up, but were under no obligation to do so, we attracted quite a bit of attention.

There are county ordinances making it illegal to go faster

108

than five miles an hour past a marina or where boats are kept stored.

Out in the open, it is courteous to slow the boat to the same five miles an hour when going past moored boats. And this is particularly true when the boats are tied fore and aft parallel to a bank in a slough.

A wake makes waves and waves cause a boat to rise and fall. If two boats are tied together—even when they are separated by bumpers—the action of a wake can cause quite a bit of heavy thumping.

So we went slowly past the boats in Steamboat Slough and on down this beautiful waterway.

At times, we would find people camped along the bank, having only a small boat with an outboard motor and sleeping bags. At others, we would pass really palatial cruisers. And, of course, there were all sorts of the various types of boats in between.

Then we came to a place where there were camping grounds and tents under the trees. People were fishing, catching their breakfast, or taking an early-morning swim.

By this time, the sun was considerably higher and we were able to cruise at speed, slowing down whenever we came to a boat which was moored and slowing down when we passed or met other boats.

There were clusters of boats here and there along Steamboat Slough, although this was the middle of the week. During the weekend and the long holidays, it is pretty well filled.

Then we were out of Steamboat Slough, into the Sacramento River, down the river, into Threemile Slough, through that to the San Joaquin River, on into False River, and then down the west side of the submerged Frank's Tract in what is known as Piper Slough.

Dick DeShazer knew some people he wanted us to meet, Jiggs and Estelle Thrush, who run the Bethel Harbor marina; and we were fortunate enough to find them home.

109

I understand that Thrush was a successful businessman who retired and came to Bethel Island to take a good long rest. His business instincts and his genius for constructive work, however, are such that he started fixing the place up, then building a marina; and now he is in the midst of a full-scale, highly successful operation.

He is philosophical enough not to let anything bother him; and he and his wife and their dog, Maggie, all came down to sit on the shaded deck on the River Queen with us and visit for an hour or so before we reluctantly parted company.

There is something about big-caliber people which carries a stamp of authenticity just like the word "Sterling" on silver; and the minute one meets Mr. and Mrs. Thrush, one knows that these people *really* rate.

In my business, I collect characters just as some people collect postage stamps and, despite the fact I had thought I was in more or less of a hurry when we moored at the Bethel Island marina, we had to tear ourselves away when it came time to depart.

We stop to visit Jiggs and Estelle Thrush. (L. to R.: Dick DeShazer, Jean Bethell, Estelle Thrush, the Author, and Jiggs Thrush.)

There is at least one Chinese junk on the Delta.

The east side of Bethel Island is just about one long procession of marinas and we had to creep along at a rate of five miles an hour for miles, but it is interesting to look at the various boats that are in the covered berths and to note the interesting names painted on the sterns.

One boat is called *Sogozit;* from time to time one sees other humorous names, such as *Mama's Mink.*

There is even at least one Chinese junk in the Delta (I think there are others) made in Hong Kong, shipped over by steamer. The one I saw, is a typical junk and, I am told, is carefully made from the finest materials.

I have cruised along these docks many, many times, but I always like to sit back and watch the various boats as we glide by, and see the activity along the waterfront.

Moving slowly, one has a chance to see things which otherwise would escape notice.

For instance, there are the professional catfishermen. I call them professionals because they are nearly always sitting in the same places on the same docks, fishing for catfish—and, I presume, catching them.

These people are hardy, tough, resilient individuals who have, for the most part, reached an age when they have either passed the bibilical three score and ten or are close to the mark.

They seem to be a remarkably healthy lot. I don't know whether their rugged good health is because they spend so

"Johnny" Johnson shows how he acquired the nickname of the Catfish Kid.

JOHNNY JOHNSON
CATFISH KID

much time in the open air, or because their diet, as far as protein is concerned, consists largely of native catfish. Perhaps it is a combination.

I determined to get in touch with at least one of these individuals and find out, so to speak, what makes him tick; and since it was going to be necessary for us to wait over a short time at Bethel Island and since one of these typical catfishermen in the person of Hubert (Johnny) Johnson hangs out at DeShazer's docks, I determined to get acquainted.

Johnson is somewhere in his seventies. He has a leathery skin, a raw-hided, muscular frame, keen but deep-set eyes, and a face which has all the wrinkles of a contour map of the Yosemite Valley.

Johnson is up at daylight every morning and out on the boat dock catching catfish. Apparently, his diet consists largely of catfish.

On talking with Johnson, however, it turns out that he is much concerned with the number of other people who are catching catfish and the diminishing supply of the fish. "Several thousand additional people each year are dragging catfish out of the Delta sloughs," Johnson insists. He feels that the legislature should establish a season on catfish.

Johnson may have something, but human nature being what it is, Johnson apparently wants the conservation to start with the other guy. Johnson spends a good part of his day fishing, and I know that there are times when he catches more catfish than he could possibly eat. At such times he is generous in giving the fish to his friends, but the idea of throwing a catfish back into the water after he has caught it is entirely foreign to his way of thinking.

Sam Hicks and I love to fish, but there is something lovable about the catfish that keeps us from killing them.

I think part of this respect and admiration for the catfish comes from his willingness to fight to the last ditch. There is no give-up in a catfish.

113

"Johnny" Johnson, the Catfish Kid.

114

When we first came to the Delta, we caught a mess of catfish, killed them, skinned them, fried them, and ate them. They were delicious.

The next time out, I caught a catfish and when I went to open his mouth to take the hook out, he clamped his jaws shut, looked me right in the eyes with his little, defiant catfish eyes, and made up his mind that if I wanted to get his mouth open I would damn well have to pry it open by the use of superior force.

And pry it open I did. I finally got my thumbnail past his lips and, by working the thumb, managed to get the jaws pried open.

All this time the catfish was trying to hook me with one of his sharp fins.

The catfish has needle-sharp bones in the big fin on his back and the two fins on each side. He is, moreover, adept at flipping his tail so that he can catch the hand of an unwary fisherman and slap it against one of these needle-sharp bones, which, in turn, are coated with a sort of slime which is mildly poisonous to the human system. A catfish wound will smart and burn something like a bee sting.

This particular catfish hated to give up. When I finally had him held in such a way that he couldn't move his body, holding the fins so that the sharp points were between the openings in my fingers, when I had the forefinger of my right hand down his throat so that I could disengage the hook, he still didn't quit. He looked me in the eye and gave a deep-seated contemptuous croak.

I told Sam. "That settles it. We aren't going to kill any more catfish."

So, Sam and I threw this catfish back, took pliers and files and filed all the barbs off our hooks so we could catch catfish without hurting them.

We purchased a wire basket which hangs down in the water so that catfish can be held in the basket without harm, and

Larry Hughes demonstrates the way to hold a catfish.

from that time on whenever we caught catfish we would put our catch in this basket. Then when we got ready to leave we would bring the catfish up out of the water, photograph them, and turn them loose.

The "professional" fishermen regard this as an act of sacrilege.

Sam always gets a kick out of asking Johnson how many catfish he has caught, and then when Johnson tells him, asks him how many he has turned loose.

The question is always good for a sharp reaction. Johnson stiffens as though someone had jabbed him with a pin, and says indignantly. "*I* don't turn catfish loose!"

Johnson has had quite a variegated list of experiences. Among other things he was the head barber in one of the exclusive San Francisco clubs, and he has cut the hair of

116

many a celebrity—Governor Hiram Johnson, President Herbert Hoover, United States senators, famous athletes, writers, cartoonists, and a host of millionaires.

Moreover, Johnson has a keen, retentive memory and is bubbling over with anecdotes.

In fact, the Delta country is fairly well filled with remarkable characters.

I don't know why this is true, except that perhaps the Delta country offers a human eddy in the stream of civilization. Men who rebel against the routine treadmill of civilized existence disengage themselves from the rapidly flowing current of hectic activity and come to rest in the slack tides of the Delta regions.

There is an opportunity here to live a life of individual

Helen King and a basket of catfish.

initiative. One can just about set his own pace and, by catching and eating catfish and bass, one can keep a fairly high protein diet with virtually no cash outlay.

Moreover, the salty characters who make up the life of the Delta consist not only of the frugal individuals living on pensions, but retired businessmen—some of whom are quite affluent—active merchants who like the environment of the Delta, men who like the water and quiet living, men who are practical philosophers.

Among these outstanding characters whom we met in the Delta, Raymond Stagg is one of the most picturesque.

A born showman, Stagg is endowed with more than the ordinary amount of intelligence. He is a keen observer, a quick thinker, and he has parlayed his talents so that he can now have just about anything he wants out of life.

A one-time newspaper artist, he drifted into operating a gambling house in Reno and used his sales talents to such good advantage that, while he enjoyed the relatively low rental of a place two blocks out from the main streets, his showmanship was such that he was dragging in the business.

For a long time Stagg had been interested in the Old West, in guns, in ammunition, and in shooting. When he became interested in gambling, he had a remarkable collection of rifles, pistols, and shotguns which attracted people to his place of business in droves.

The result was that the now famous Harold's Club bought Stagg out and arranged to employ him for a period of years as its publicity director.

Stagg's flamboyant publicity attracted people by the thousands. With the long hair of a Western scout, Stagg's appearance commanded attention. Both Stagg and his wife would engage in match and trick shooting which left the audience breathless.

Nor were their spectacular successes the result of chance. Endless preparation and practice as well as skill went into the

118

The Author and Raymond Stagg.

handling of the guns. Stagg managed to mix brains with gunpowder and so had a distinct edge over his opponents.

In those days the match muzzle-loading rifles were loaded with semismokeless powder which Stagg found left a moist residue in the barrel and, to be certain that his own powder charge got down to where it belonged without sticking to the sides of the rifle barrel, Stagg used a copper tube which was completely dry on the inside. Moreover, he carefully cast his bullets, then finished them by hand, weighing them on gold scales so that each of his bullets had *exactly* the same weight.

Even today, in his early eighties, Stagg has long hair braided in a queue at the back of his head. His Western hat, his keen eye, his whole bearing stamp him unmistakably as an outdoor character.

While he was advertising Harold's Club, Stagg had an automobile completely circled with an ornamental strip of silver dollars. He felt that silver dollars were just about the best advertisement he could give for Harold's Club, and when he attended public gatherings, he carried huge bags of these silver dollars and, from time to time, tossed a handful out into the crowd. He was careful to get the older silver dollars so that many of the recipients found the dollar they caught bore their birth date.

Today, Stagg lives on Bethel Island in a house overlooking one of the main channels. His mind is as sharp as ever, his eyes are remarkably penetrating and keen, and he needs no glasses.

People who know him well talk in awe about the man's uncanny financial sense, his ability to gauge trends in the real estate and stock markets and in the financial fluctuations of the business world.

It is dollars to doughnuts that if just the right deal came along requiring unconventional, flamboyant publicity, a shrewd business sense, and the touch of a master, Stagg would forget all about retirement and be out on the firing line with a brass band hanging up new records.

120

Another interesting character is Edwin H. Vose—better known all over the Southwest as *Chuckawalla Slim, the "Rockologist."*

"Chuck" or "Slim," as he is known to his friends, moves about, taking his trailer to the desert in the winter, up to the Delta in the summer. From time to time he takes little buying or selling trips. In the meantime, Chuck and his wife lead as nearly a carefree existence as one can imagine.

I first met Chuckawalla Slim fifteen or twenty years ago when he had his trailer in the desert and I happened to stop by.

His trailer, with its sign CHUCKAWALLA SLIM, THE ROCKOLOGIST, is a combined house with living quarters, salesroom, and showcase. How he manages to utilize every inch of space is amazing.

The walls are lined with little glass-covered cabinets, below which are drawers partitioned into lined, square receptacles, and everything is filled to the brim with gem rocks, semi-precious rocks, gold ore specimens, fire opals—in fact, you name it and Slim has it.

Some of these specimens are exceedingly rare and presumably very valuable.

One large chunk of fire opal which Slim has had for years he values at five thousand dollars, and it is a spectacle of breathtaking beauty.

Chuckawalla Slim has lived an interesting life, a life of complete independence, when one considers the regimentation which is the usual lot of so many men so much of the time.

Chuckawalla Slim is a self-educated man and, by that very token, in many ways one of the best philosophers I know.

The story of how he got his start in life is fascinating because I think it is highly significant.

We talk from time to time about opportunity knocking at the door.

As I look back on life, I think opportunity keeps a veritable tattoo of knockings at the door. If we are sitting in our chairs, wrapped in lethargy and feeling sorry for ourselves because

The Author and Chuckawalla Slim, the Rockologist.

122

we don't have the things we want out of life, we don't hear the knocking. But, if we are active and go to the door every once in a while, I think we will find opportunity standing on the threshold more often than we realize.

I have learned a lot about life and about human nature from owning boats.

We keep our boats at Remsburg's by the bridge crossing to Bethel Island, and there are literally dozens of boats moored side by side in these spaces. I started checking on who had these boats.

It is surprising to find in how many instances a person who is engaged in some routine occupation had an opportunity to branch out in some little sideline which showed unexpected possibilities, and developed those possibilities until he found himself in a very lucrative business.

For instance, think of the diaper service which has now developed into quite an industry. For how many years was an opportunity of this sort knocking around undeveloped, simply because nobody happened to think of it?

Or, getting closer to home in the Delta, take the houseboat rentals.

A short time ago a good rental houseboat was virtually unheard of. I think perhaps it was the income tax that started the whole deal, rather than any human ingenuity.

I think perhaps the first person to rent a houseboat was a man who had expert income tax advice and who found out that, if he would rent his boat for a few weeks during the summer, he could then make it a commercial deal and write off all his depreciation, upkeep, etc., and have the boat for eleven months out of the year on a deductible basis.

This man soon found that the rental was exceedingly lucrative, decided to buy another boat and keep it on a rental basis for added income. So, almost overnight, the houseboat rental business sprang into existence on a commercial basis.

In the case of Chuckawalla Slim, the opportunity which knocked at his door was completely disguised.

123

Chuck got his start from a mess of discarded, culled peas. That is an unusual way for a man to get a start. Opportunity knocking at the door in the guise of discarded peas is hardly to be expected. Chuck certainly didn't expect it.

On the other hand, I have a feeling that if Chuck hadn't got his start from the discarded peas he would have found a start from some other source, and without too much delay.

Chuck has been one of the most successful men I know of. He has been able to be his own boss, he has built up a business which has made him well-known and given him a good living. He has been acquiring knowledge every day of his life. He has made a host of friends. He has just about everything he wants out of life and he owes it to his ingenuity in recognizing opportunity.

Chuckawalla Slim, the Rockologist, didn't realize opportunity was going to knock when he got his load of culled peas.

He was down in the Imperial Valley during a period of unemployment. He had a makeshift camper automobile in which he had a gasoline stove, a bed, some pots and pans, and not much else.

Slim heard that the canneries in the Imperial Valley were buying peas by the ton. They were canning these peas, and the canned peas were of a fine uniform grade.

Slim started thinking. He knew that nature didn't grow peas in a uniform grade. He knew that there were small peas and large peas.

What became of the small peas?

Slim determined to find out.

He drove to the canneries.

In those days there was nothing they could do with the culls except throw them away. Slim asked if he could have some of the discarded peas. He was laughingly told to take all he wanted.

Since the peas were free and Slim was hungry, he took a lot.

Slim went down to the railroad station, parked his car, and

started to cook the peas. There was a patch of shaded lawn by the railroad station, and human derelicts who "rode the rods" as well as people who were out of work rested up by reclining in the shade of this lawn, using the toilet facilities of the railroad depot and, in general, waiting for "something to turn up."

Slim cooked his peas. There were plenty of them. "I didn't have any milk," he says. "I didn't have any butter, but I had salt."

So Slim decided to share his peas with the unfortunates who were sitting around on the lawn.

He took out dish after dish of peas and the men devoured them, getting caught up on fresh vegetables and nourishment at the same time.

A man was sitting on a bench watching, and Slim offered him peas.

"No, thanks," the man said. "I didn't come out here to get something to eat. I came out here looking for help, and you're the man I want."

"What sort of help?" Slim asked.

"I want to hire a cook," the man said.

Slim laughed. "I know nothing about cooking."

"You're not talking to me," the man told him. "I've been watching these men eat. Whatever it is you're feeding them, you've certainly cooked it so it's a savory repast."

"These men are hungry," Slim said.

"My customers are hungry," the man told him.

"I can't cook at all," Slim said.

"You can cook for my customers," the man told him. "I'm running a hunting club. When they get up in the morning, they're too sleepy to know what they're eating, and when they come back at night, they're too hungry to give a damn what's put before them. You're hired."

So, Slim found himself a job, thanks to a little ingenuity and a mess of peas.

Slim went out on the job and kept his eyes open.

125

When his boss went from the duck club to a nearby town to get some provisions, he passed a place where there were unusual rock concretions of various shapes. He put a few of those in the back of his pickup.

Once when he and Slim were in town a senator from Texas rather patronizingly wanted to know how much these concretions would amount to and had his chauffeur start to unload them.

Slim's boss was an independent sort of a cuss and he told the senator they weren't for sale. He turned down a rather fabulous offer because he didn't like the man's approach.

Slim decided that if a Texas senator wanted concretions of this sort, there might be something in it. So Slim started picking up concretions.

It wasn't quite as simple as that because it needed a lot of salesmanship to go with it, but Slim's active imagination furnished the salesmanship in the form of an attractive verbal background and, in the course of time, Slim had built up quite a good business in concretions.

Then along came a man who had a lot of very high-grade rocks which would take a polish, and wanted to trade some of his rocks for some of Slim's.

Shortly after that Slim was in business.

He's been in business ever since.

"Chuckawalla Slim, the Rockologist," is essentially a desert rather than a Delta character; but, during the summer months when it is hot in the desert, Chuck and his wife migrate up to where they can enjoy the cool breezes of the Delta and stay there until fall.

As Chuck expresses it with a smile, "I have a bird brain" —then he goes on to explain that birds have sense enough to go north in the summer and south in the winter and he does the same.

Chuck makes the birds work for him in another way. They give him some interesting articles of sculpture.

126

Chuckawalla Slim displaying his bird sculptures.

Chuck takes loaves of stale French bread when they have become hard as bricks and puts them out on a table. The birds come and peck on the bread, and when the loaves are about half consumed they have usually assumed the proportions of modern sculpture—the bottoms, of course, being flat. Sometimes the finished result bears a startling resemblance to a symmetrical work of art.

At this stage of the game Chuck takes the loaves into his trailer and puts out others for the birds to work on. At times he will show credulous tourists his remarkable stale-bread sculptures and listen to their "Ohs!" and "Ahs!" of admiration. Then he will perhaps explain how it all happened.

More and more people are beginning to appreciate the beauty of semiprecious gemstones—including different types of agate, lavic jasper, the jade which is found in a few places in the United States, some of the more colorful grades of petrified wood, and dozens of other beautiful rocks which take a high polish and can be used for earrings, costume jewelry, and bolo ties which seem to fit right in with a Western outfit.

And strange as it may seem, despite the beauty of these rocks, they are comparatively cheap. This is because they are found mostly by prospectors who go out and collect their own specimens, do their own polishing, and have a relatively small overhead. These prospectors then "trade" their rocks. People like Johnny Woodworth of Paradise, California, who specializes in gold, and "Chuckawalla Slim, the Rockologist," whose real headquarters is in a trailer park near Indio, deal direct with many sources of supply. There are few middlemen in the rock business.

Rock collectors all over the United States know Chuckawalla Slim and his distinctive trailer, and Slim knows rocks. He can take a look at about any semiprecious stone and tell what it is, where it came from, and what it is worth.

He started out to prove the old prospector's adage that gold is where you find it, and Slim has specimens of just about every known type of rock with rich streaks of visible gold running through them. Amassing this collection is a tribute to his powers of perspicacity and patience.

Since Chuck is an avid reader and has one of the most retentive memories I have ever encountered, Slim is today a well-educated, practical philosopher. His memory is absolutely astounding. He remembers every little detail about his meetings with various people, remembers their problems, their tastes, and much about their general background.

Some ten years ago when Sam Hicks stopped by Chuck's trailer house in the desert, Chuck had been quite hospitable

128

and Sam had given him a bit of unusual rock he had been carrying.

Today, Slim still has that bit of unusual rock in his pocket. He startled Sam by pulling it out of his pocket. "Remember this?" he asked.

Slim keeps a scrapbook of varying things which have interested him, the usual number of newspaper write-ups, showing him as a colorful character, etc., etc., photographs, and occasionally some interesting bit of information.

Slim wanted to show me his scrapbook, and looking through it, I found it an interesting compilation.

Then I came to a half page of single space typing.

"Read that," Slim said.

"What is it?" I asked.

"My grandniece, Cindy," Slim said, "wrote this as a short story. She was fourteen when she wrote it. Read it."

I read it, and then I read it twice.

Slim was chuckling. "They *all* read it twice," he said.

I read it a third time, and then I told Slim, "You have got to do something with this. This is the most unusual short, short story I have ever read in my life."

Here was a half a page containing in just about two hundred words the most gripping, unforgettable short, short story I have ever encountered.

With Slim's permission I made a photocopy of the page and tried to interest an editor, who is a friend of mine, in the story.

This editor was interested in the story all right but didn't think it was suitable for his magazine.

I didn't want to let the matter rest there. I told Slim I thought the story should see the light of day and suggested making a financial arrangement so that I could publish it in this book.

Remember that this story was written by a young girl, fourteen years old, a girl who is too young to have developed any artificial literary technique, a girl who wrote from instinct, from the heart, or perhaps from the soul. And perhaps from some instinctive knowledge which is denied to us oldsters.

We are reminded of the words of the poet, "The youth who daily farther from the East must travel still is Nature's priest and by the vision splendid is on his way attended." In any event, I am setting forth this short, short story, written by a remarkable youngster.

Read it once and you'll read it twice. Read it twice and you'll never forget it.

Here is the story:

MY SISTER
by Cindy

Nan, my little sister, and I came here a lot so I guess that is why I came. There she is, in the clearing. I like watching her like this. She does so many things on her own now.

Nan is quiet and shy. I guess I was, too. She is my copy, you know, at least that is what they said. But I had green eyes instead of blue. My hair was blond like hers but it turned dark brown, hers will, too, maybe red when she is older. I will have to wait and see.

Is that her singing? She sounds more grown up since I left. I remember when I used to start off and she would join in. One of us was always off key. I think it was me but we did not care.

At night she would get into bed with me and tell me all kinds of stories. I only believed half of the things she said but it was funny anyway.

I think I miss her the most. Mom and Dad some, but they were always gone somewhere. I hope they take better care of her, now that I have left. Mom cried a lot at my funeral, so I guess they will, but I will stay close to her, just in case.

130

Edwin H. Vose, better known as "Chuckawalla Slim, the Rockologist."

CHAPTER SEVEN

Unusual Animals Live in the Delta

The Delta is remarkable, not only for its scenery and its people, but for its animals, and perhaps the attitude which the people have in dealing with the animals.

Take, for instance, Stan's Market.

This is one of the two very exceptional markets on Bethel Island.

Both are in rather unpretentious buildings as seen from the front, but they are pack-jammed in the interior with a surprising assortment of high-class groceries.

Bearing in mind that these are local centers of supply for the hundreds of yachtsmen who come pouring into the community on weekends, particularly during the vacation months, one realizes that a market, in order to remain in business, must have a good assortment of quality merchandise.

A person who has fifteen, twenty-five, or thirty-five thousand dollars tied up in a yacht is apt to be accustomed to the best and when he goes out on a cruise and provisions his boat, he naturally wants to get the highest quality money can buy.

For that reason, both markets are, in my opinion, exceptional, and are particularly noted for the quality of meat they sell.

It is no great trick to get Grade A meat that will cook up quite tender, but to get meat that is of just the proper age so that it has just the right flavor requires skillful buying and a good source of supply.

Before he sold his market, Stan owned a dog, or rather the market owned the dog, or it might be more appropriate to say the dog owned the market.

It was *not* Stan's dog. It was *not* the market's dog. It was really the dog's market and yet, what with the state law and provisions of sanitation having restrictions in the matter, the dog couldn't come into his market.

How the dog happened to adopt the market, no one knows. Presumably, he was a stray from somewhere, but he adopted the market. He felt that the market belonged to him.

From time to time, Stan would take a piece of meat scrap and come to the door to give it to the dog. The dog accepted it, but quite apparently considered it not as meat that Stan gave him but as meat that the market gave him.

The dog kept constant watch over that market day and night. He knew he couldn't go in the place, but nevertheless that market was his.

Some months ago when a gang of men tried to break into the market, they reckoned without the dog.

It was the dead of night, but the dog was still guarding the market.

The men started to cut a hole in the window, and the dog went after them, barking hysterically, screaming for help, until the neighborhood was aroused and the men fled, with the market sustaining no more damage than a broken window.

This dog wouldn't make up with strangers. He didn't want to be petted. He didn't want anyone to come near him. He would be at the entrance to the market, and when he saw a customer coming he would courteously step to one side. He seemed to realize that it takes patronage to keep a market going.

It's hard to tell whether Stan's Market belongs to the dog or the dog belongs to Stan's Market.

134

But this was the dog's market. It was not Stan's Market, it belonged to the dog, and Stan humored the dog in this respect, kept him well fed and quite content.

There is another outstanding animal in the Delta country, a dog owned by Harold and Carol Taylor at Tiki Lagun.

Those of you who read *The World of Water* will remember that the Taylors bought the land on which Tiki Lagun is now located. There was an old barn on the place, and, for the most part, the land had been used as a dump heap. The Taylors, with very little outside help, went to work, cleaned the land up, then started constructing floats and covered berths for boats. They drove themselves unmercifully, but they accomplished unbelievable results. And, today, Tiki Lagun is one of the gem spots in the Delta, with an attractive eating place, ample parking facilities, and a long line of covered berths.

Anyone who wants to see the Delta country should by all means stop for a while at Tiki Lagun and then make the four- or five-mile run up the Stockton Channel to Stockton.

The channel from Tiki Lagun to Stockton is a remarkably interesting ride in a boat. There are miles of navy ships in mothballs. There are beautiful mansions with well-kept lawns running down to the water's edge. There are country clubs, boats, and docks.

Harold and Carol Taylor are the sort of people you refer to as being "my type of person." They have a high-class trade in their marina and in the restaurant they have opened up. The grounds are beautiful. They are completing a parking place, a place for trailers with showers and toilets; and by automobile they are only a few minutes' run from Stockton. They are perhaps a mile from the Stockton Channel on the body of water known as Turner Cut, shortly before the place where it runs into Whiskey Slough.

To me the interesting thing about their place is that it represents the good old American pioneering spirit and shows what can be done with will power, elbow grease, and

135

two-fisted determination. They have taken what was a dump heap and made it into a beautiful marina, and they have done it by hard work with their two hands. Every time I see the place I am surprised at the extent to which they have carried on their improvements and the general atmosphere of quality which permeates the place.

The Taylors have a collie named Piper, one of the most intelligent, well-mannered dogs anyone could ask for.

Sometime ago, a woman appeared with a dog that had evidently been pretty well pampered. She felt certain that the collie would "jump" on her dog and injure it, so she insisted on keeping it on a leash.

The dog didn't like the idea of a leash and, taking advantage of a moment when his owner's attention was diverted, she gave a sudden jerk, pulled the leash loose, and went rushing down the marina.

Piper had been lying down in well-mannered self-effacement, but was keeping an eye on proceedings. Suddenly, she was off like a shot, chasing after the other dog. The woman screamed in terror.

The collie ran up to the other dog, grabbed the end of the leash in her mouth, turned, trotted back with the woman's pet, and gently deposited the leash in her hand.

There is yet another story to be told about Piper. The Taylors recently bought a horse for their daughter and staked the animal out on a tie rope. The dog picked up the end of the tie rope and wanted to play tug-of-war with the horse.

The horse promptly proceeded to follow the dog with all the docility of a well-trained horse. Piper looked back, saw what was happening, and almost dropped the lead rope in surprise. Then she proudly elevated her head and tail and proceeded to lead the horse around the stretch of lawn in front of the main house at Tiki Lagun.

The Taylors had another unusual animal, or rather an unusual combination of an animal and a bird.

136

The Taylors have a collie, Piper, shown here with Jean, their daughter.

When they took over the place, there was an old ramshackle barn which had to be torn down.

The barn held a kitten which they adopted, and also held a pigeon which had no place else to go, so it just stayed around.

It seemed that the pigeon and the kitten had become well acquainted and, as they grew up, the acquaintanceship ripened into a deep friendship.

The kitten wanted to play and, having no other playmate except the pigeon, the two struck up an arrangement by which they played together all over the place.

Carol Taylor says that it was terrifying to watch. The cat would swarm all over the pigeon. The pigeon would beat the cat with its wings and then they would roll over and over until finally the pigeon, tiring of the procedure, would fly up on the roof and sit there smiling down at the cat.

Once the cat, trying to get a good hold on the pigeon, took the pigeon's entire head in its mouth.

137

Either the pigeon suddenly mistrusted the motives of the cat or thought perhaps that feline instincts might make the cat go too far.

The cat was simply holding the pigeon's head loosely in its mouth, dragging it around, but it was a situation where the pigeon evidently figured that an ounce of prevention was worth a pound of cure.

The cat suddenly spit and jumped backward with its tail bushy and its back arched, and the pigeon flew up to the roof and sat regarding the situation with smiling condescension.

Carol Taylor is certain that the pigeon took the cat's tongue in its sharp beak and gave it a good nip.

After that, in playing, they simply rolled over and over and jumped and leaped and cut up all sorts of antics, but the cat showed no desire to take the pigeon's head in its mouth.

Dick DeShazer has a very remarkable German shepherd who is trained as a watchdog.

Quite frequently, at night, Dick will take the dog out for a stroll in order to "button up" the place.

Any friend of Dick's is perfectly safe, but woe betide any prowler who might be on the dock tampering with any of the luxurious houseboats which Dick keeps on display.

This dog loves the water, but once, plunging in water, got an infection in its ear.

No one knows how a dog could connect the two in his mind. He may have heard the veterinary explaining to Dick that it was bad for a dog to get water in its ears. Regardless of how it happened, the dog learned its lesson in one session.

Now, the dog will walk gently down a launching ramp, get into the water and swim, with his head and ears well out of the water. Then he will come back and climb out, careful to keep his ears dry. But under no circumstances will he repeat his former habit of running and jumping into the water.

Animals generally have a lot more intelligence than people realize.

CHAPTER EIGHT

"Whoopee"

As I have previously pointed out, yachtsmen are gregarious, and there is a species of camaraderie which it is difficult to define.

For instance, a group of people will rent a rowboat at one of the resorts. They may or may not be affluent enough to rent an outboard motor at the same time. They may decide to rely on oars and muscle as a means of getting where they want to go. They will take the boat a couple of miles out in the tules, tie up, and start catfishing. A fifty-foot luxury cruiser, resplendent with chrome and mahogany, obviously owned by somebody with money to burn, will come gliding by, and it is not at all unusual to see the man behind the wheel of the power cruiser give a friendly wave of the arm to the occupants of the rowboat—the friendly greeting of one yachtsman to another.

And when one passes out of the main channels into the fishing sloughs, the big cruisers are usually as careful as anyone else to slow speed to a crawl as they go past a boat which is anchored so that the wake will not disturb those sitting in the anchored boat.

This sense of fraternal companionship exists in the various covered moorings which are in reality a long, floating shed—

several hundred feet long, divided into berths for the boats, covered with a heat-reflecting roof and a floating walkway. This furnishes a shelter which is apt to be cool in summer and warm in winter, since water is a great air conditioner.

Most of the boats which are moored in these covered berths are homes within homes, as well as a home away from home. They contain living quarters which vary from the extreme miniature to the relatively commodious proportions of the house cruiser.

As a result, the people who stay at these covered berths get to know one another and get to like one another.

There is an unwritten code which covers the etiquette of living in these berths where a cruiser costing fifty thousand dollars may well be berthed within a few feet of one costing a fifth that much. Yet such is the freemasonry of yachting that people who share the rows of berths and have the same interests in common form weekend friendships.

One yachtsman will never force his way, never intrude upon another yachtsman. They exchange greetings; they may spend the weekend within ten feet of each other, living on their boats. They have an ideal social relationship, something like that of people on a luxury cruise who occupy adjoining deck chairs.

The occupants of one cruiser may decide on a cookout, and since it is considered poor business to have a charcoal fire on the wooden deck of a gasoline-laden cruiser, the barbecue coals will be in a portable metal container out on the dock in front of the boat.

People passing by will pause for an occasional comment on the aroma of the steaks. There may be a bit of banter, but no one intrudes upon the privacy of the other and there is the fellowship of perfect understanding.

The primary reason for this, of course, is that, taken by and large, yachtsmen are mighty decent people. And, since they are actuated by the common motive of wanting a floating

A float with joyous dancing girls in the procession which went out from Tiki Lagun.

home away from home, each is quite apt to understand how the other feels.

Harold and Carol Taylor, who own the resort and covered berths at Tiki Lagun, decided on an experiment last September in order to see to what extent people who were using their facilities would like to associate on shore on a fraternal basis.

In front of the restaurant and social hall at Tiki Lagun is an expanse of lawn running down to the water where the mooring sheds are located.

So the Taylors decided to give something in the nature of a community barbecue for all the people who had boats at Tiki Lagun. The idea was that they would have a celebration and sell tickets for a meal, with a social cocktail party where each yachtsman brought his own supply of liquor.

Since the motif of Tiki Lagun is South Seas, it was decided to have not a conventional barbecue but a Hawaiian luau, and then plans began to grow so that it included entertainment, replete with dancing girls in their native costumes and Hawaiian decorations.

141

The Taylors located a caterer, or barbecue expert, who specializes in that sort of thing, Robert Swahlen of Gilroy, and Swahlen agreed to furnish all the meat the guests could eat, cooked in real Hawaiian fashion.

So the pigs were cooked over hot coals buried in the ground, as nearly as possible in a genuine Hawaiian manner, and the whole Saturday afternoon and evening was turned into one gigantic celebration.

It was an unqualified success.

Enough tickets were sold so that there were plenty of funds to do the thing in grand style, and the yachtsmen seized upon the idea with eager avidity and turned out to help in the celebration.

In no time at all a big barge was fixed up with Hawaiian decorations and colored lights. The owner of one of the River Queen house cruisers installed loud speakers for a hi-fi program of Hawaiian records, and those who had boats at Tiki Lagun turned out with a will. A whole procession of boats accompanied the barge and paraded up the channel to Stockton, whistles tooting, pennants waving, while on the barge comely girls in native costumes danced the hula with such perfect rhythm that the whole performance became breathtaking.

The yachtsmen had the time of their lives.

Because I had cruisers berthed at Tiki Lagun, I was included in the invitation, and I, in turn, invited Dick and Moyne DeShazer to be my guests. So, the DeShazers, Jean Bethell, Sam Hicks, and I had a thoroughly enjoyable time.

As it happened, the weather was perfect and we gathered on a high point of land to watch the returning cruise as it came in from Stockton.

Everyone was in the highest spirits. The girls were dogtired, but so exhilarated that whenever the Hawaiian music started, the shimmering, transparent garments began to undulate in time to the Hawaiian melodies, and then they were off on another hula with yachtsmen clapping hands, shouting greetings to those on shore, and in general having a fine, hilarious time of it.

Then followed the "social hour" on the lawn with everyone mindful of the fact that the invitation had provided "B. Y. O. B." (bring your own booze), but everyone was fully aware of the great natural law that it is more fun to share than to keep.

Old friendships were renewed. New friendships were formed. A stage was fixed up at the social hall, there was more Hawaiian music, beautiful, graceful dancing, and, as the evening progressed, lighting effects which enhanced the artistry of the costumes.

Then the pigs were dug out of the ground, smoking hot, thoroughly cooked, moistly tender and juicy, and everyone sat at a long table and gorged. The caterer had guaranteed each ticket holder all he could eat.

Some of the Hawaiian dancing maidens at the celebration at Tiki Lagun.

Taken by and large, the affair was such a success that the Taylors are planning to stage a repeat performance.

We have formed interesting friendships in our mooring berths. Our "neighbors" are always ready to give us a hand at any time we need help when coming in on a difficult wind or tide, and are always willing to share information about conditions they have encountered in cruising the various parts of the Delta country.

The demands on my time are such that I can't retire. I have combined offices and residences in five house trailers, which I keep at Dick DeShazer's trailer park within a few hundred yards of where most of my boats are moored. For the most part, I am able to work in the mornings and cruise in the afternoons, but there are times when the pressure of work is such we must work during the long and sometimes very hot afternoons.

At such times it is a pleasure to transfer our activities down to one of the house cruisers where the steel body is cooled by the gurgling waters, where the deep shadows of the place make one feel that the whole dock is air-conditioned.

Because I am trying to find out all I can about the Delta and about boating, I have several different types of boats in addition to those I've already named.

One of my latest acquisitions is a knockaround boat, built along the lines of what I call a sea scooter, because when the boat gets up and starts planing along the surface of the water it seems to be like some huge scooter.

This boat is a Ken Craft, powered with an outboard motor. It is in the shape of an oblong with everything in the open— in fact, I can't describe it any better than as a sea sled.

The point is, however, that it is unsinkable, the body having been engineered so that even with people aboard and a hole punched in the hull it is going to stay afloat under all conditions. It is light and maneuverable and can be used for running errands, fishing, exploring, and for photography.

144

The Valco cruiser and the Whit-Craft as seen from the bow of the River Queen.

Eventually, when I finish exploring the Delta and writing about it, I will have to settle down and sell off some of my boats, but in the meantime I have a variety of waterborne facilities for fast exploration, for comfortable living, for fishing and photography.

And is it fun!

145

CHAPTER NINE

Back to Snodgrass Slough

Dick and Moyne DeShazer are ideal vacationing companions.

During two years' cruising with them under varying vicissitudes and conditions I have yet to hear them exchange a cross word. Their comments are good-natured, humorous, and founded upon a perfect mutual understanding.

I like to travel. I like vacation living, but I also like all the comforts and conveniences. Therefore, the house cruiser is just about the most perfect way of vacationing I have been able to find.

I can get in one of my house cruisers and inside of ten or fifteen minutes I am out where I have complete privacy and good fishing, where I can relax away from the sound of telephones, where the only people I will see are those of my own choosing and the yachtsmen who pass by in the middle of the channel.

What more could anyone ask of life?

When we are out overnight we follow the custom of putting all the women on one boat and all the men on the other.

In this way, the women can sleep late if they wish. They have no need to bother about modesty in close quarters. If

146

Dick and Moyne DeShazer, listening to the Author tell a lurid
anecdote . . .

*. . . are mildly
amused and
a bit
shocked . . .*

*. . . then
overcome by
the punch line.*

147

We kept the two house cruisers moored sufficiently far apart so the women weren't kept awake by our penny ante.

they want to watch television programs, they have Moyne's transistor-powered color television set.

On the other hand, the men on the other boat can do just as *they* please.

If we track dirt into the place we can sweep it up when we get darned good and ready. If we want to rinse out the coffee cups without using a lot of hot water and detergents and polishing them till they shine like crystal, that's our privilege.

We get up and lounge around in pajamas, and if we feel like it we play "penny ante."

It makes for an ideal existence.

In the summer of 1964 we had spent a good deal of the time camping in one place (Snodgrass Slough). The next year we wanted to see new country, wanted to do more adventuring. So again, we started out with the DeShazers with two house cruisers and with the old dependable Smith Craft, now equipped with a Homelite motor, and the sea scooter, or Ken Craft, which was to prove so much fun.

In the intervening time, my book had been published and had attracted enough attention to make a pronounced difference between the two trips. In 1964, we were simply several more yachtsmen. The following year, we were all generally recognized. People would hail me by name and occasionally tell us that they had learned about the Delta and had decided to come there from reading my book.

The River Queen moored at one of our camps in the Delta.

As a result, on the later trip, we saw more and more rented houseboats and talked with quite a few of the happy vacationers who were enjoying themselves in the Delta country.

In addition, we now had old friends in the various resorts along the banks of the sloughs.

I am particularly partial to Giusti's, one of these resorts, because it is so conveniently located, is such a nice place, and because the owners are so thoroughly hospitable.

The whole crew at Giusti's is well known and universally liked. Mention its name to a yachting crowd and the faces of people light up.

There is something of the old type of hospitality about Giusti's which makes the visitor feel he is not a customer but an honored guest.

The bar is quiet, dark, and air-conditioned. The dining room has uniformly good food at very reasonable prices.

The place is small enough so the cooking has a home flavor. Everyone is made to feel at home.

"Mo" keeps exploring around and knows just where to go to get garden-crisp vegetables for the salads, the best of meat for the entrees, and at the start of the meal, the waitress brings in a great tureen of hot soup from which the diners can serve themselves. There is a distinctive flavor about the food which speaks of unremitting care in its preparation.

Sam Hicks pilots the Smith Craft.

Taking on gasoline at Giusti's.

On this trip we explored down or rather up the Mokelumne River to the New Hope Landing and Café.

This place is only a little over a mile by water, or perhaps not that far, from Giusti's through a channel where the scenery is photogenic with its stately trees leaning out over the water casting reflections, and dark pools of restful shade.

At the New Hope there is a café where one sits some twenty or thirty feet above the water and looks out of picture windows. When I ate there I had a very good steak.

I believe the kitchen adjoins the downstairs restaurant because the waiter came up, took our orders, then departed and returned after a while with the food. Eating in the upstairs rooms was an enjoyable experience. We sat by the window

151

The tower at Locke is actually over 1500 feet high.

and looked down on the channel and the dock. Between bites of food and sips of chilled beer we watched the boats coming in to the dock to be gassed up—and it is a pleasure to "size up" other boaters, to watch the way they approach the dock, how they handle the lines.

One of the distinctive landmarks of this part of the country is the Locke-Walnut Grove television tower.

This tower is a long, slender needle of steel rising an incredible fifteen hundred and forty-nine feet above its foundations. It is held in place by steel cables and is so high that the spectator is simply unable to believe what he sees.

The function of this tower is to relay television programs, and there is a huge catwalk platform on the top.

"Mo," of Giusti's, has been up to the top and says it is a

152

never-to-be-forgotten experience. I saw some of the colored .35 mm. slides he had taken from the top of this tower and became dizzy simply from looking at them on the screen.

Along the Delta country there are similar smaller structures which are, I presume, only a couple of hundred feet high which are used to suspend electric cables as they cross the waterway.

There is an interesting story in connection with these smaller towers which I have as yet been unable to verify, but which is given to me by the old-timers as gospel.

It seems that at the time these towers were built there was a federal regulation providing that structures for the purpose of transporting wires across navigable waterways had to be taller than the masts of any sailing vessel which entered the San Francisco harbor.

It seems incredible that this could have been the reason for these tall towers transporting the wires across the Delta country, because the depth of the water is such that no sailing

A houseboat stops for gas at New Hope Landing.

"Mo," of Giusti's.

154

vessel with a mast anywhere near that height could have possibly sailed up these sloughs. The fact remains, however, that these towers, apparently of a uniform height, transport the high-tension wires across the sloughs.

Seen from a distance, the television tower at Locke seems to be just a little taller than these other towers, but seen close at hand, the vision is awe inspiring.

"Mo," describing his trip up the tower, says that after you have completed the first three or four hundred feet of the journey, you look down and it seems that it is absolutely impossible for the tower to be any higher. The slender tower fades away down below in perspective to a veritable pencil point, yet you realize there are more than a thousand feet of tower up above you.

I have been up in the Eiffel Tower and thought that was quite a thrill, but ascending this television tower at Locke would be ten times the thrill that a person would get going up the Eiffel Tower—at least it would be to me.

Apparently it takes a lot of red-tape unwinding for anyone to get up in the Locke tower. "Mo" thinks that it might be arranged for me, but after looking at his photographs I think I am doing all right looking at the Delta country from the hurricane deck of a house cruiser.

On our various trips to Snodgrass Slough I was not only in search of material for a book but also looking for complete relaxation. I wanted to get into the black bass fishing grounds, catch some, cook them, eat them, and I wanted to camp up in The Meadows for a while. I also wanted to try to get some striped bass.

There are many different kinds of fish in the Delta, but it is best known for its striped bass, and these fish are delicious eating. They are also full of fight. Even when a small striped bass ten or twelve inches long takes your hook, he does it with the sort of strike that one would associate with a fish two or three times its size.

However, I may as well admit right at the start that as far as I am concerned, there is no thrill in bass fishing which can compare with the complete relaxation of leisurely houseboating. My intentions were good, but the cold, hard facts are that I didn't so much as put a bass lure in the water.

I am not certain I know why this was the case. I know that I intended to, but I lost all sense of the passing of time and absolutely all sense of urgency. I was willing to loaf and fish for catfish, but casting a plug for black bass was doing it the hard way, and I didn't feel like doing things the hard way.

When I made my first house cruiser trip in 1964 we had spent quite a bit of time on Snodgrass Slough. As it happened, Jerry and Doris Waterworth had their home on the opposite side of Snodgrass Slough—right across from our boats.

From time to time we would see Jerry Waterworth out in the evening, catching a mess of catfish, and gradually we became acquainted with him and then met Doris; eventually we all became firm friends.

Jerry Waterworth has a string of gasoline stations and has a terrific natural talent as a painter. He can sit down and knock off portraits which are exceptional, but he "doesn't have time" for painting and looks on what is a very remarkable talent as being something hardly worth mentioning.

His wife is a charming woman who has the advantage of being easy on the eyes.

After we got to know them we invited them to a barbecue, running over and picking them up in the Smith Craft, bringing them across to the uninhabited island where we had our boats tied up, and having some of George Marr's steaks barbecued by Sam Hicks.

When we went back up to our old camping grounds in Snodgrass Slough, we tied up the boats where we had spent so much time earlier and again had the pleasure of renewing our contacts with the Waterworths.

It was a real thrill being back at the old camping grounds

and, naturally, we spent some time in recalling incidents of our former trips; but it had been an active day and before very long we were in bed, Jean and Moyne in the River Queen, Dick, Sam, and I in the Whit-Craft.

We turned off the generators and moonlit silence descended on the placid waters.

Within a matter of minutes I was wrapped in the warm, refreshing blanket of deep slumber.

Once or twice I awakened to hear the lap of the water, to roll over, burrow into my blankets, and again drop into blissful oblivion.

Finally when I awakened to broad daylight, Dick had the percolator on and the delightful aroma of coffee was permeating the cabin. I dressed, had coffee with Dick, then heard Sam talking and went on deck to find that he was carrying on a conversation with a bass fisherman who was drifting gently along, casting a plug along the shore.

I recognized this man as Lee Ewoldt, whom we had met on our trip the previous year.

Ewoldt lives an ideal existence. He is a lover of fishing and fishing tackle. He has a rod and reel shop in Sacramento, repairs and sells tackle, and two or three mornings a week gets up early to drive down the few miles to Snodgrass Slough, where he invariably catches a nice string of black bass. Unusually he is back on the job by ten o'clock in the morning.

Here is a man who has a genuine love of fishing and of the outdoors and his hobby keeps him healthy.

Ewoldt came aboard for a cup of coffee and a little chat. He had a nice string of bass with him, and he had the usual fisherman's story of the big one that got away.

Only this time the story was really something, because Ewoldt, who is a veteran fisherman, was convinced that he had a world's record bass on his line. He got a glimpse of it once or twice during the fifteen or twenty minutes he was

The roots were intertwined like serpents.

playing the fish; then the fish broke the tackle and escaped. Ewoldt is completely satisfied that if he had been able to land it he would have had a record black bass.

After Ewoldt left, Dick and I planned to go out and cast a plug, but we just couldn't get up the energy.

I felt as if it were a summer Sunday morning and I had nothing to do but relax in the shade and read the papers.

We were tied up to huge trees whose roots intertwined like serpents—trees which cast a deep shade over the boats and over the water. We had very comfortable chairs to sit in, the decks were cool, and the air was soft and caressing to the skin.

I had had a wonderful night's sleep; I was completely

rested and relaxed. We had had a nice breakfast. I didn't have to do anything except what I wanted to do, and I didn't want to do a darn thing.

Later on, I did go with Dick, Moyne, and Sam in the sea scooter down into the backwaters where the slough was literally choked with water hyacinths, but I'm glad to state we didn't even take a fishing rod with us. We simply sat there perfectly still in various choice spots and, after a few minutes, watched the black bass come to the surface and begin to feed on something on the underside of the leaves of the water hyacinths—presumably some insect life palatable to them.

We stayed in Snodgrass Slough for a couple of lazy days and then moved up into The Meadows, a distance of perhaps two or three miles.

During the height of the season The Meadows is pretty well lined with cruisers as it is a beautiful, sheltered place to tie up, with plenty of calm water for fishing and swimming, and tall trees casting cool shade.

We tied up to huge trees.

People who rent houseboats tend to get as far as The Meadows and then, somehow, just settle down. Probably because in all the Delta country there is no more beautiful scenery and no waters which are more peaceful and sheltered.

We had a couple of light boats with us for running errands, the big Smith Craft, and the Ken Craft, or sea scooter.

Once when we had to go down to Giusti's to use the telephone we took both boats and left one of them tied up for Mo, Dolores, and Irene Giusti to use in coming that evening for a barbecue with us.

We were tied up at a sandy beach under the trees, where we spread out comfortable chairs and had charcoal-broiled steaks, baked potatoes, a salad, and an ice-cold watermelon.

"Mo," who is an experienced boatman and knows every inch of the Delta country, insisted that he could get his family home even late at night with perfect safety—what's more, he did it. But don't ask me *how* he did it because he started out in darkness when I wouldn't have gone a hundred yards.

Tense with excitement, a water skier glides by our boat.

The Ken Craft—a type of sea scooter.

Nor did he want to use the spotlight which was on the boat, but preferred to let his eyes get accustomed to the darkness and follow the channels the several miles which stretched between our camp and his dock, using only the red and green running lights.

It developed that Irene Giusti has a phobia about boats. Despite the fact she has spent her life on the edge of the waterways, this was the first boat ride she had ever taken— and I think it did her good.

We gave her a lot of kidding about it, told her we'd have her water skiing on my next trip.

It seems incredible that one can form such close friendships in such a short time. A little over a year ago I hadn't known the Giusti family. Now we had all the warm intimacy of old friends.

The Whit-Craft towing the Ken Craft.

This is in part because the Delta people are the salt of the earth, and in part because of the influence of houseboating. And, of course, because we met these people at a time when everyone was free from tension. It is at such times that we have the ability to relax and enjoy our friends and their companionship.

The Delta nights on that trip were little bits of paradise. Dick had brought along a projector and a collection of his colored slides. Jean had some of her colored slides. We put up an improvised screen and had picture shows in which we relived some of the adventures we had had together hunting lost mines in the desert, exploring the wild places of Northern Nevada, navigating the beautiful tree-lined channels of the Delta country.

162

A year earlier, when I had been writing my first book about the Delta country, I had been looking for adventures, something out of the ordinary to write about. Now, I was content simply to relax.

I had been troubled with hypertension and had been forced to take some of the tranquilizers which have been developed by modern medicine.

In my particular case, these tranquilizers not only slowed me down somewhat but, unfortunately, acted on me in about the same way as if I had given up smoking. I began to put on weight, and I kept putting on weight. No matter what I did, I put on more weight.

However, it appeared the tranquilizers were necessary in order to combat the strain under which I was being forced to carry on my rather complicated business affairs.

In this second Delta vacation trip I went out for an avowed rest. I wanted to get away from everything just as much as possible. I wanted to relax, to do nothing, to eat, sleep, and watch the birds in the trees.

To the surprise of everyone, myself included, and particularly my doctor, my blood pressure promptly dropped thirty-five points.

Sometimes when we have exhausted the artificial means, we find that going into nature's storehouse gives us just what we need, and we only have to reach out and take it.

CHAPTER TEN

Policing the Waterways

From time to time we would run across a sheriff's boat patrolling the waterways.

At first I thought these boats were largely decorative and the deputies in charge had something of a sinecure, but one day we engaged John Walsh, a deputy of the Contra Costa sheriff's office, in conversation and invited him aboard for a cup of coffee.

There was a little chill in the air, and having been patrolling for hours in an open boat, Walsh welcomed the idea of a hot drink. He tied his boat alongside ours, so that he could hear the radio calls, and sat in for a coffee and conversation.

That was the start of an interesting association which ripened into a friendship with Walsh and with another deputy, George Halter.

What we found out about police work in the Delta caused me to revise my opinions materially.

Law enforcement has to go on a twenty-four-hour-a-day basis, and law enforcement in the Delta includes a variety of problems, rescuing persons who are drowning, trying to find the bodies of those who have drowned, getting data on collisions, occasionally helping out a disabled boat, as well as all

164

the rest of the things which are common to law enforcement on the mainland.

Unfortunately, no matter how many warnings are given, people will disregard those warnings. They overload boats; they operate boats too fast around blind corners; they go swimming without realizing the force of the tidal currents; they lose their heads when they get in a jam, and instead of drifting with the tide, expend their strength in a frantic effort to swim against it. They will eat a heavy meal, then go swimming. They sit perched precariously on the edge of a boat and then when some unexpected wave causes the boat to lurch, they go overboard.

People who can't swim disdain to wear life preservers. People who can swim underestimate the strength of the current. All of these things contribute to tragedies in the Delta.

The big bugaboo of the Delta, however, is fog.

Several times a year a thick, fine-grained fog, known as the

John Walsh, the deputy sheriff, comes alongside on one of his patrols.

Al Doreo, a state game warden, drops in with Deputy Walsh for a visit.

"tule fog," settles over the entire Sacramento and San Joaquin Valleys and stays sometimes for two weeks at a time.

During those times air service is interrupted, automobile accidents pile up on the highways, and, in the course of time, the cold, damp fog seems to penetrate to the marrow of the bones.

Those are the times which are dreaded by the law-enforcement officers in the Delta, but they have to keep on the job just the same. In fact, there is even more reason for them to be out in the Delta then than in periods of good weather.

During periods of heavy fog when it is impossible to see more than fifteen or twenty feet ahead, officers will track down the sound of a motor and, coming on a boatman, will refrain from being unduly officious because every boatman who has a boat more than ten feet long fancies himself as a captain and regards his nautical judgment as infallible.

On these occasions, the officers will take the tactful approach and ask the boatman for directions, such as, "Can you tell me the way to Sandmound Slough?"—Sandmound Slough being part of the junction of two of the principal waterways in the Delta.

Nine times out of ten, the boatman will indicate a completely erroneous direction.

Then the officer will say, "It just happens I'm going to Sandmound Slough myself, suppose you just follow me."

It is bad enough to find one's way in the Delta country with its maze of connecting sloughs during broad daylight. The main steamboat channels are, of course, marked, but there are literally hundreds of miles of sloughs, old rivers, cuts, canals, and waterways, some of which are connecting and some of which come to a dead end.

It is part of the duty of the sheriff's office to enforce speed limits, and particularly to curb the careless boatman who makes a habit of disregarding the posted speed signs.

The more serious duties of the sheriff's office lie in a far different field, one which wouldn't occur to the average boatman, and I am mentioning them here because they represent a needless loss of life.

If a man is driving an automobile and has trouble, he pulls to the side of the road, steps out, and is on dry land. If a man is operating a boat and has trouble, he finds himself swept along by a tidal current or a wind, or both, and there is no place for him to stop unless he can get his boat into a protected mooring.

If a man uses his head, he doesn't have much trouble, but it is absolutely astounding to find the number of people who don't use their heads.

One big problem is caused by people who insist on going

The more serious duties of the sheriff's office.

out alone in boats equipped with highly efficient, extremely powerful outboard motors. The boatman sees something ahead in the water. He stands up in order to get a better view and finds there is a piece of ugly flotsam just ahead, a half-submerged log, or a waterlogged piece of lumber.

Almost automatically he jerks the tiller to avoid the obstacle. The boat is going faster than he realizes and the boatman is thrown off balance.

Perhaps he regains his balance; perhaps he finds himself in the water with his highly efficient outboard motor speeding the boat away from him at twenty miles an hour—and twenty miles an hour on the water can be very, very fast indeed.

If the boatman is a strong swimmer and keeps his head, and if he swims quartering with the current he may well reach shore. But if he tries to go against the current, he is going to get in trouble, and it is surprising how many people *will* try to go against the current.

168

A man is in an anchored boat, fishing, then slips, loses his footing, falls overboard, and the tide starts carrying him away from the boat. His natural tendency is to try to swim back to the boat, a matter of only a few feet.

If it is as much as twenty or thirty feet, only the most powerful swimmers can ever make it, and even those powerful swimmers have trouble when they are swimming with their clothes on. The average swimmer is doomed the minute he starts trying to fight his way back to the boat if the tidal current is running against him, and at a good rate.

Many people can't understand how it happens that there are tidal currents in fresh water. The answer, of course, is that the water comes sweeping in from San Francisco Bay on the incoming tide, flows out on the outgoing tide. The salt water represents a barrier in the lower part of the bay, and, when

The Author and John Walsh, the deputy sheriff who gave us so much information about the Delta.

State Game Warden Al Doreo with a good-sized striped bass.

this barrier is raised and lowered, it naturally affects the fresh water of the rivers flowing into the bay. So we have tidal waters long after we have ceased to encounter salt water.

Another form of accident which is far too common takes place when a man starts an outboard motor while it is in gear. The motor takes off with a roar and the man is pitched overboard.

Once when we were scheduled to meet with deputies from the sheriff's office, they were late in showing up, and their tardiness was caused by a tragic mishap.

A man, leaning over the stern of his boat making some adjustments on his outboard motor, inadvertently started the motor. The outboard motor was in gear, the boat took off with a jerk, the man went overboard and found himself standing at low tide in water a little over his waist on a sandbar out in the middle of a very wide slough.

The man's wife was in the boat without the faintest idea of how to run the outboard or how to handle the boat.

In a panic, and in trying to bring the boat around, she opened the throttle on the motor, swung the boat around so that it capsized, and the woman fell in the water and was drowned. The man found himself marooned on a sandbar with the tide coming in.

The sheriff's office had to piece together what had happened from circumstantial evidence.

The man stood his ground on the sandbar with the incoming tide sending the water higher and higher, until finally he was submerged and drowned. The accident had happened at night, and by daylight when other boats saw what had happened it was too late to do anything except notify the sheriff.

This is the grim side of boating, the tragic side, and I mention it here because it should be emphasized, and well emphasized.

Don't take chances in boats. Remember that water is deep, swift, and dangerous.

And then, of course, almost every year somewhere in the United States some careless boatman literally runs over a swimmer, and the propeller of the outboard motor cuts off the swimmer's legs or inflicts fatal damage.

Dick DeShazer tells of a wild night's adventure in rescuing a man to whom he had sold a houseboat.

The man had the houseboat moored safely alongside a levee bank. It was night. He got in a dinghy to row the few feet to shore, lost his balance, the dinghy turned over and swept him out into the middle of the swift tidal current.

The man clung to the upturned dinghy and kept air under it so it remained afloat, the man, meanwhile, trying his best to get to shore.

The current was so swift it kept him out in the middle of the channel.

It wasn't until the man had been carried through the night in the cold water for some twelve miles that he was able to get to shore at a place where he could see lights.

The lights were part of an agricultural camp and the occupants telephoned Dick DeShazer, who made a wild night ride, picked up the soaked man, wrapped him in dry blankets, and got him back to his houseboat.

His wife had been sitting there reading, thinking her husband had gone to town after provisions.

After we became friendly with the Contra Costa deputies who patrolled the sloughs, we found that they not only were real gentlemen, but that they had an encyclopedic knowledge of the waterways in their county, and Sam and I quite frequently took our Valco speed cruiser and went along with them for the purpose of meeting some of the salty characters who inhabit the little islands which are scattered through the Delta country.

In this way we met some remarkably interesting individuals and had an opportunity to see the sheriff's office at work.

As a representative of the law, the sheriff's deputy wants to

Deputy George Halter spots a submerged raft . . .

. . . tows it to the bank . . .

. . . and ties it securely.

be neatly dressed, but on occasion his duties make it exceedingly difficult to preserve a neat appearance.

Once we came upon George Halter wrestling with a piece of waterlogged wreckage which had floated out into the main channel.

Halter towed this heavy piece of wreckage to the shore all right, but then he had to hunt up some wire and tie up the wreckage so the tide wouldn't drift it right back into the channel.

Before he got done, Halter had his coat, shoes, and socks off, his clean, well-creased trousers rolled up above his knees, and he was wallowing around in the sticky mud.

However, he managed to get the job done, got his feet washed, his socks and shoes back on, his trousers again turned down and, with his coat on, his insignia of office well displayed, Halter resumed his patrol duties none the worse for wear.

It was through John Walsh that we learned of B. F. Perry and the Tennessee Red.

Tennessee Red is a variety of Eastern quail, and Perry, who is a mechanical genius, operates a marina with storage for a large number of boats.

Perry had installed a boat lift which is a masterpiece of mechanical ingenuity. The lift is a combination dry dock and elevator. It drops down below the water. The boat—sometimes as long as forty-six feet—is eased into position in the elevator; then the motors are started and the elevator raises the boat up out of the water and to the level of the machine shop where Perry does his work.

This may sound simple to the uninitiated, but when one realizes that the strain has to be equalized on each of the pulleys which do the work, that there has to be complete synchronization on each of the two sides, and that a dead weight of many tons has to be lifted safely, smoothly, and without undue delay, it becomes a major undertaking.

174

Tennessee Red.

However, Perry isn't satisfied with all this, but, in addition, he has a menagerie of cats and dogs, and pens in which he raises pheasants, quail, and quite a few specimens of rare birds.

How Perry and his wife can keep up with all these activities is beyond me, but they keep the place running as smooth as clockwork.

Now, Tennessee Red either thinks that Mr. and Mrs. Perry are two quail, or else thinks of itself as a human being. It is a little difficult to tell which.

At the time we saw the bird, it was approximately two years old and had been raised, literally, in the bosom of the Perry family.

At night, the bird sits on the back of Perry's chair while he is reading or watching television. If he gets up to go to the bathroom the bird flutters down and follows along behind him.

Tennessee Red tries to teach the Author quail talk.

No matter where the bird is, if Mrs. Perry reaches down and makes a scratching motion, the bird comes running in order to see what "Mother" has uncovered for him in the way of a delicacy.

But as far as I am concerned, the most interesting thing is the bird's attempt to teach the Perrys quail language.

And it has been remarkably successful in its instruction.

The bird can fly and it can run like a greyhound, yet the Perrys take it out and turn it loose on the lawn or on one of the picnic tables and the bird talks to them incessantly, apparently acting on the theory that constant repetition will gradually get them to understand quail talk.

And the Perrys have learned to understand a great deal of this talk.

176

For instance, when I was photographing the bird, it kept making a series of peculiar sounds which the Perrys seemed to have little difficulty in understanding.

Perry said first, "It wants something."

Mrs. Perry had tuned her ear to the continuing sequence of little plaintive chirps and said, "Yes, there's something it wants."

"Sand," Perry said.

And sure enough, the bird wanted sand. The Perrys took it over to a levee where there was quite a bit of sand and the quail had an ecstasy of enjoyment in a dust bath, scattering the warm sand up over his head and through his feathers, fluffing the feathers, then shaking them, spreading its wings and relaxing in the sunlight.

After a while the Perrys told the bird it had had enough and took it back to the picnic table, where the quail made little chirping sounds which even my uninitiated ears inter-

Perry's propeller shop, showing the interesting electric "lift" by which cruisers can be lifted from the water for repairs.

preted as sounds of contentment. And then, as they gradually became slower and a trifle lower, I correctly interpreted them as meaning, "Go away now, I want to sleep. Try not to disturb me."

And the bird stretched out on the table, rolled over to one side, put its legs out, regarded me with sleepy eyes, then drifted into relaxed slumber.

Perhaps animals can talk, perhaps they can't. But we do know that they can tell a lot about the emotions of a human being from the sound of his voice. A good dog can tell just about what his master is thinking, presumably from the sound of the voice rather than the words.

I can readily see how birds, with a series of chirping in different keys and different pitches, can tell each other various things, certainly when they want something, when they are contented, when they are alarmed, when they are upset.

In any event, Perry and his wife have accomplished a great deal in learning to understand quail talk.

CHAPTER ELEVEN

Salty Characters

On one of our trips with the deputies we had been introduced to Capt. Lester W. Salisbury, an old-time river tugboat captain, a member of a group of old-time seamen who referred to themselves as gas-skinners, who was living all by himself in a bachelor's cabin far down at the other end of the Delta country.

Salisbury and his wife had retired and lived an ideal existence. His wife, however, had passed away and Salisbury had been left with his faithful dog, Red, his memories, and his house.

He hadn't wanted to leave the house where he had been so happy, and he felt that his dog couldn't adjust himself to the ways of civilization. The dog had never known any life except on the little island where they were living. So Salisbury geared himself to the tempo of a solitary life on the island and stayed on.

We had only met Salisbury briefly but, in that time, had found out he was a storehouse of information relating to the old days on the rivers. So, after our houseboats had been tied for a while in The Meadows, we decided to take a long trek and go down to the southern end of the Delta country.

Captain Lester Salisbury and his dog, Red, have a perfect understanding.

The distance was probably not over forty or fifty miles, but since we were going to tow the Smith Craft and the sea scooter, we intended to travel at a leisurely pace, resting, relaxing, and boating all at the same time.

We needed some service on the Whit-Craft and, for a while, considered going back to camp at Bethel Island, staying there for a day, then starting out the next day for the southern part of the Delta country. However, we were both afraid of what might happen if we got back where Dick could be reached by long-distance telephone calls and confronted with all the things which had been piling up during his absence. Also, because we needed that extra day, Dick arranged to have one of his men bring another River Queen down to meet us and take the Whit-Craft back to be serviced.

This was done and we made the second part of the trip in two River Queens, looking as identical as peas in a pod. We made the jump in a leisurely fashion, eating lunch while we were under way.

As we had hoped would be the case, Salisbury was the soul of hospitality and invited us to tie up at his floating dock and make ourselves right at home.

I think he was glad to have an opportunity to visit with people, and he certainly was cooperative in explaining some of the things we had been wondering about and telling us something of life on the river many years ago when millions of tons of freight were shipped back and forth by barge.

Salisbury's island is separated from the mainland by fifty or sixty yards of water and he goes back and forth in a rowboat. He keeps a car parked on the mainland side and, from time to time, drives in to the nearby town of Tracy for provisions.

His life is one of extreme simplicity, in that his wants are simple and yet he lives like a king.

The River Queen in front of Captain Salisbury's cabin.

There is a levee, of course, protecting the island and Salisbury has built his house on this levee, carefully utilizing every foot of the raised ground and planting his yard with fruit trees so that he has a cool, shaded walk in the summer and lots of fresh figs in season.

Then he has landscaped the water side of the levee and put in a substantial mooring float.

Salisbury has his license as a tugboat captain which was renewed every five years, and his last renewal was number eight, meaning that for forty years he was licensed to move cargo in the Bay area.

This sounds simple, but it is far from simple. One doesn't just take hold of a barge and start towing it.

Take a boat weighing eight or ten tons which is moored at a dock and if you want to move it you have only to take one hand and give it a slow, steady push. The boat moves a fraction of an inch, then an inch, then to the limit of the rope

Captain Salisbury shows the Author a tree that was gnawed down during the night by beavers.

which is holding it. The first part of the motion is very slow; the last part will show a steady increase.

Then take hold of the boat and try to stop it. You can exert your full strength, but the boat keeps moving slowly for an appreciable distance before it can be brought to a stop.

Now that is essentially the problem of towing loaded barges in the Delta country.

While the weight of barges can furnish resistance in the form of inertia, there is virtually no friction in the water itself. Therefore, within limits of motion, it takes only a small steady force to get a mass of great weight moving through the water.

Once that weight starts really moving, however, it has such a momentum that a heavy barge could crush a boat like an eggshell.

As long as a tugboat captain can keep this momentum working in his favor he is moving along, going where he wants to go, but if that momentum ever gets at cross-purposes with the tugboat, the tugboat is helpless. Or, as the rivermen say, "in irons." One gathers that getting "in irons" is the nightmare of the tugboat captain. When that happens, as a last resort, the only thing to do is cut the towrope so the tugboat can be freely maneuvered.

However, all this was to come later. We got down to Salisbury's place in the late afternoon, tied up, and found that Dick's crew had brought our automobile down and parked it alongside Salisbury's car so we could cross a relatively few feet of water, step in our automobile, drive to Tracy, replenish supplies, pick up mail, then return in a few minutes to our hideout of shaded seclusion.

On weekends some of Salisbury's family usually visit him, and since it was a Saturday when we arrived, his daughter and his granddaughter were there with him. We had a lot of food so we invited them all for dinner aboard the house cruisers.

These are the aspects of life on the river which I like, visiting with different people, being able to entertain, yet being completely mobile. We could stay there with Salisbury as long as we wanted. On the other hand, we could untie the ropes and be gone in ten minutes, and when we left we could go less than a mile, tie up under some overhanging trees, and again be lost to civilization for as long as we wanted.

When Salisbury had retired and built his little house on the island, he settled down to comparative quiet and happiness. Because he had been born a little too soon he missed the so-called "fringe benefits" which are so much a part of present-day employer-employee relationships. He does, however, have a very small monthly income and the surprising thing is that with that income he has been able to live a life of complete financial independence.

The automobile which he drives to Tracy for supplies is certainly not of the latest vintage. The rowboat with which he crosses the channel is propelled only by a pair of weather-beaten oars. His dog is well fed. He has electricity on the island, a big electric refrigerator, and a radio which enables him to receive the calls of "hams" from all over the country.

However, Captain Salisbury doesn't do very much running around; a very occasional trip to Tracy for supplies represents the extent of his travels.

In the days when he had been a tugboat captain, one of his closest friends had been Captain Quinn, who also ran tugboats in the Delta country and who had also retired, and, as it turned out, was also living on an island.

It was an irony of fate that Quinn and Salisbury lived for a year within a mile or so of each other on their respective islands without visiting for the simple reason that Salisbury didn't have any idea where Captain Quinn was located, and, with only a pair of oars to furnish his power for the rowboat, Captain Salisbury wasn't doing very much exploring, and Captain Quinn didn't know where *his* old buddy was located.

184

This is a good illustration of the isolation of the Delta country.

We took Salisbury in our Valco up to Quinn's place within a matter of minutes and had a nice visit with the Quinns.

Salisbury had had a working partnership arrangement with the Quinns during the period when commercial catfishing was legal in California.

The stories of commercial catfishing stagger the imagination.

At times, Salisbury grossed a thousand dollars a week, and he had caught and processed as much as fourteen hundred pounds of catfish in one day.

The Quinns with the Author.

The so-called "processing" of catfish is quite a job.

The amateur fisherman with a catch of six or eight catfish finds himself pulling, twisting, and trying to get the slippery skin removed so he can prepare the catfish for the frying pan.

Everyone agrees that the way to prepare a catfish is to hold its head firmly in place, preferably by nailing it to a board, and then skin the fish with a pair of pliers. The trouble is the pliers get covered with slime and slip off the skin, and, in general, handling a wet catfish in order to prepare him for the pan is almost as much of a job as it is to catch the catfish in the first place.

A person who is processing fourteen hundred pounds of catfish in a day, however, can't afford to waste any motions, any sympathy, or any effort. The catfish are handled on an assembly-line basis.

When we got Captain Salisbury together with the Quinns, it was, I believe, the second time they had been together in years and they had a wonderful time sitting there and reminiscing about the old days while we sat with our eyes and ears open, listening to the stories of what was virtually another world and another life.

In those days merchandise of all sorts was shipped all over the river and the sloughs. Great barges were stacked with farm produce, manufactured merchandise, and machinery, and transported to the marketing centers.

Captain Salisbury told us of barges so loaded with baled hay that it became necessary to put one pilot house on top of the other so that one could see over the hay; of loads so heavy that against the tidal current the tow was only capable of making two or three miles per hour; stories of navigating heavy loads through dense fogs.

That is a thing which I simply can't understand.

During the days when the weather was clear we went back and forth through the thousands of interconnecting sloughs, and I don't think Sam Hicks ever has failed to know exactly where he was and what turn to make, although I confess that at times I was pretty much confused and sometimes down-right disoriented.

However, we don't have any tows. We have very mobile boats which can be maneuvered easily and rapidly. When we approach an intersection, we can slow speed and get out pretty well in the middle of the intersection before commit-ting ourselves to the turn.

I get goose pimples when I think of trying to do this in a heavy fog; and when one is navigating through a heavy fog with a string of barges in tow—well, I just don't want any part of it.

Yet this has been so much a part of Captain Salisbury's life that he would like nothing better than to be standing in the wheelhouse of a good tugboat with a string of barges in tow, dense fog surrounding him, groping his way through the fog with a whistle and with echoes, figuring tidal currents and speeds, running compass courses and chugging his way up the river.

The thing which ruined river transportation, Salisbury says, was the construction of highways and bridges, with bridges the worst of all.

When I first knew the country, the automobile road from San Francisco to Sacramento was one which entailed two rides on ferries.

The roads were generally narrow and relatively rough in spots, and driving from San Francisco to Sacramento repre-sented quite an investment in time and patience.

That was why so many people who were bound for the Northwest or on transcontinental trips East loaded their cars at the ferry building on one of the big Sacramento riverboats, had a nice dinner, went to sleep in a well-appointed state-room, and awakened in the morning to find their car parked on the dock in Sacramento ready to be driven away.

As far as the movement of freight by truck was concerned, there was no possible way in which the trucks could compete economically with the barges.

Then came the construction of bridges, the widening of highways, the improvement of trucks, the development of diesel motors, and now suddenly the barges are all but a thing of the past. And the highly specialized knowledge which Captain Salisbury and his kin had acquired has become a store of useless information.

It would seem, however, that once tugboating gets into your blood it is in there to stay.

One of Captain Salisbury's most prized possessions is a colored photograph taken of a big sailing ship which has been towed out of the Delta country, has cleared the Golden Gate, and is standing away with all sails spread, at a point apparently just outside the three-mile limit.

Salisbury can take that picture and point out significant things about the boat, the sails, the rigging, which the ordinary observer would never notice.

Another one of Captain Salisbury's prized possessions was one of the most unique horseshoes I have ever seen, and that horseshoe, in itself, tells a story.

As I said earlier, the history of the Delta country goes back to the very early days, the days before there were diesel engines, trucks, or roadbuilding machinery. The levees were built by hand, by Fresno scrapers, by Chinese coolie labor, and by horses.

The horses slipped and bogged down in the soft mud, so it became necessary to invent a species of mud shoe for the horses, and heaven knows how they trained the horses to wear those shoes.

Digging around in an island levee, making repairs, Captain Salisbury came upon one of these shoes.

Its purpose is quite evident from an inspection of the shoe, but how it could have been durably attached and how a horse

Lester Salisbury, his dog Red, and the horse's mud shoe—a relic of bygone days—which he found embedded deep within the levee.

could have been trained to use it without falling all over his feet is another question.

This shoe goes far, far back to a bygone day when the fields were swarming with Chinese coolies working frantically on the construction of levees, when a "two-horse-power" scraper meant exactly what it said, two horses as power.

We had an idea of how times had changed when we were within a few miles of Captain Salisbury's island. A huge "clamshell" dredge was towering in the channel, its derrick high above the trees growing along the bank.

The clamshell bucket, weighing heaven knows how many thousand pounds, would be lifted over a spreading fifty-year-old tree, would drop down, crushing the tree into a shapeless tangle of limbs and splintered wood; then the great bucket would open, clamp around the trunk of the tree, and lift the tree out by the roots as though it had been pulling a weed out of a garden.

One of the big dredges being towed up the river.

The bucket would then drop the tree, dip down into the slough, and come up with a great load of dripping mud and silt which would be placed over the hole where the tree roots had been, over the splintered mass of tree limbs. Then again the bucket would lower, come up with another load of mud for the top of the levee. Then the barge would move along and start smashing the next tree.

In the days of hand labor, cutting that tree would have been quite a job. Pulling the roots out of the ground would have been a physical impossibility. Getting mud from the bottom of the channel to put on top of the levee would have been virtually out of the question.

That dredge and barge represented the utmost in efficiency, and the finished product represented the sacrifice of rustic beauty to modern engineering methods—methods which many a rancher along the waterways feels are a big mistake, and all yachtsmen deplore as the destruction of nature's beauty in order to satisfy paper standards of statistical efficiency.

We stayed there at Captain Salisbury's island for a couple of glorious, carefree days.

It turned out that Salisbury is very much of an artist with the accordion, and he played for us. He has a wonderful touch and his fingers fairly fly over the keyboard.

One night we went up to his house to visit him, to listen to his accordion playing, and, in between times, to listen to anecdotes about the old days on the river. The hours of the night slipped away so that it was later than I realized when I stole a surreptitious glance at my watch, but Salisbury seemed to be enjoying himself and it was a pleasure to see his eyes light up when he would talk about the "old days" on the river, of some of the more difficult and, at times, downright dangerous jobs he had performed.

Of course, looking at it in one way, a person can say these

old rivermen are living in the past, but, looking at it in another way, they have perpetuated the past into the present. Their lives are a composite whole representing the changing period of river transportation and the present-day enjoyment of modern conveniences which enable them to live simply and happily, calling on memories which are just as much a part of their lives as is the present.

No comments on Captain Salisbury would be complete without mention of his dog, Red.

Since Salisbury's wife passed on, he has had Red as his constant companion, and the depth of understanding between man and dog is uncanny.

On this first trip we got to know Red. On subsequent trips the dog became our friend and does his part to extend a dignified but cordial welcome whenever we drop in for a visit.

Came the inevitable day, however, when scripts had piled up, when it was necessary for me to get back for an extended session on the long-distance telephone, and get my dictating machine in action.

We said reluctant farewells, untied our house cruisers, hooked the lighter boats on behind and, one at a time, pulled away from the hospitable float, waving farewells to our host until we rounded the first bend, and the calm, reflecting waters of the slough hissed past the prows of our cruisers as we headed back on the long trip to Bethel Island.

The Author fishing from the Smith Craft.

Chuckawalla Slim shows his sculpture to Anita Haskell Jones and the Author.

Houseboat refueling.

The Author and J. W. Black bait their lines.

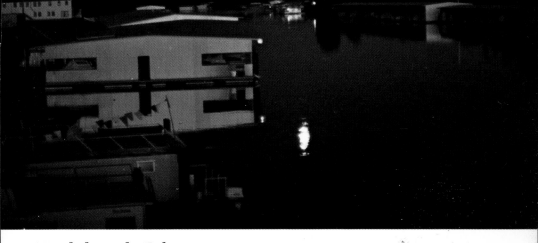

Moonlight on the Delta.

The Ken Craft in motion.

Relaxing in the shade.
Sails furled, a ketch passes through a drawbridge.

CHAPTER TWELVE

People, Dogs,
and Strays

People in the Delta country are divided roughly into two classes, the residents and the weekenders. Or perhaps one should say the boaters.

The boaters come pouring in in droves over the weekends, and these include the boat renters, people who rent the small fishing boats with outboard motors.

There are, or course, boat owners and boat renters during the middle of the week, particularly during the vacation season when boating is a family sport, but for the most part on the weekends the little communities are doing a land-office business with a vast influx of people.

It is only after one lives in the community day after day and gets to see the people who live there that one comes to appreciate its character.

No one in the Delta country is getting rich, and this particularly applies to the people who keep the small shops, but these people have sterling qualities which give one renewed faith in the American heritage and the American background.

For the most part the yachtsmen are mighty fine people. They go out on their yachts, are steady, responsible, and considerate. But there is a percentage of "tourists" who come in to spend the weekend and apparently do nothing except sit in the bars, loaf around the waterfront, clutter up the scenery, and use the weekend congestion as an excuse to dump stray animals.

This situation is true all over the country, but it seems to be particularly prevalent at such communities as Bethel Island, where stray dogs and cats are found as an aftermath of the weekend influx.

Presumably these people have a warped reasoning which enables them to say, "I'll just take the family pet out and leave it by the roadside in the country where it will be sure to find a good home."

If these people lived away from the city for a while and saw the number of pets that are abandoned in the course of the year, they probably would think a little more logically.

At my ranch in Temecula we have from three to eight dogs,

There are many boaters who bring the family and put up tents during the vacation season.

and have had for the last twenty-five years. Every one of these dogs has been a stray, abandoned by someone who took that means of giving his dog "a good home."

There is nothing more pathetic than to see a loyal animal by the side of the road patiently waiting for its master to return.

There was one case where two young dogs were dropped right by the side of the highway. After a couple of days when they had been without food and presumably without water, some of the good-hearted neighbors tried to pick them up, but the dogs would have none of it. Whenever a car stopped they would look anxiously to see if it contained their master, and when they found it didn't they would run away into the brush where they couldn't be caught.

At the bait shop at Bethel Island just where the bridge crosses over Dutch Slough, there is a dog that has been waiting for his master for some three months.

The owner of the bait shop adopted him and sees that he is well fed and taken care of, but the dog insists on waiting outside, watching each car that goes by, hoping that it will contain his master.

Since the dog had a tendency to run out and hopefully inspect every car that stopped, and since there is a lot of traffic on the road, the owner of the bait shop had to chain him up in a section of the sidewalk where he can watch each car but where he is safe from being run over.

When we stopped at the bait shop there was something about our car which evidently reminded him of his master's car. He jumped up and ran forward to the edge of the chain, whining in eagerness; then, as he got a look at the people emerging from the car, his tail drooped in disappointment. He looked at us for a few seconds, then turned and walked back to lie down with his back against the wall. Here he waits, day after day, week after week.

Such loyalty after a period of three months is indicative of the devotion that animals have for masters who all too frequently are not worthy of any part of such loyalty.

Anyone who knows and loves animals realizes that many, many times dogs and horses have character personalities which are far more stable than those of the "owner."

In fact, if a man wants to be fully worthy of the loyal devotion of a good dog he has to live up to a code of ethics which is pretty apt to make a better man out of him.

Here the dog waits day after day, week after week . . .

. . . and occasionally gives a cautious greeting.

One of the most interesting stories I have ever encountered was told by a traffic officer who was patrolling a highway on a hot summer day.

After he had been on the road for a while he decided to check on an important boulevard stop where quite frequently motorists, seeing no one coming, sailed blithely through the stop signal.

In order to check this boulevard stop the officer brought his car to rest in the shade of a tree at a wide place in one of the connecting roads and took out a pair of binoculars which he used to check the license numbers of the cars failing to make the stop, so that when he took after them and caught up with them he was certain he was tagging the right car and the right driver.

While he was sitting there he saw a car which acted very suspiciously. The driver was driving slowly along a creek road which led into one of the roads at the junction.

The officer put the binoculars on the driver and, to his surprise, recognized him as his next-door neighbor.

The driver of the car found just the right place, brought the car to a stop, jumped out of the car, opened the trunk, pulled out a sack, ran down into the stream bed with the sack, dropped it in the shade of a tree; then ran back to his car, jumped in, and drove away at high speed.

Naturally, the officer wondered what had happened. He went over to the place where the other had stopped, went down, opened up the sack, and looked inside.

He found a mother cat and six nursing kittens.

The officer picked up the sack, put it in his own car, used his siren for clearing the road, drove at high speed to his neighbor's house, ran around to the back door, carrying the sack, dumped the mother cat and six kittens out on the back porch, wadded the sack under his arm, and then went about his business as though nothing had happened.

It was years before he heard any sequel to the story. Then, at a time when people were recounting unusual experiences, his neighbor told solemnly of a phenomenon that he could vouch for and yet which was a physical impossibility.

In an awed tone he told about how he had taken a mother cat and six kittens and decided to leave them where the mother cat could "shift for herself." He said he had picked out a place where he felt there would be lots of mice, had placed the feline family in the shade of a tree, and had driven thirty miles back home, only to find when he got there that the mother cat, with the six kittens, was lying purring in the sunlight on the back porch—manifestly a physcial impossibility and yet he was able to vouch for it.

The traffic officer never said a word. If the man who got rid of the cat and kittens happens to read this, it will be the first intimation he has ever had of what actually happened.

There was a long Indian summer during the early fall of 1965, and we continued the boating season well into the late autumn.

Because I was working on scripts I would "steal" a day or so at a time, sometimes a whole day, a night, and two-thirds of the next day.

On such days we would lead a gypsy existence. Jean Bethell, Sam Hicks, and I would take the River Queen and start out aimlessly, not knowing where we were going and not giving a hoot. We would travel where the spirit moved us, at whatever rate of speed would give us good steerage way, while letting us glide through the water leaving very little wake behind us.

Sometimes we would tie up, look in the food compartment for whatever we wanted in the line of lunch, and after a lazy afternoon, return to our mooring about dark. Sometimes we would tie up, have dinner on the boat, roll into our bunks at an early hour, and have a long peaceful night of deep sleep.

On one of these gypsy trips when we had the time available we went down to say hello to Captain Salisbury and his dog, Red.

"Welcome home," Captain Salisbury said, "welcome

home!" Then he looked at Red, nodded his head, and said to us, "I had a feeling that you folks would be down here, either today or tomorrow, but I didn't want to tell Red because I was afraid I might disappoint him, and you know how it is with a dog, it's so hard to explain to him when he thinks people are coming and they don't show up."

Red was very dignified in his greeting, but very cordial. He was unmistakably glad to see us.

Captain Salisbury had said, "Welcome home," and Red adopted much the same attitude. We were no longer visitors. We were part of the family.

Always at night Red sleeps by the side of Salisbury's bed, but this night he became uneasy. He gently placed his paw on Salisbury's body and whined softly.

Salisbury let him out and that was what Red wanted. He spent the rest of the night lying where he could keep one eye on the boat and one eye on the house.

It is remarkable how much intelligence dogs have.

They don't know anything about higher mathematics because higher mathematics wouldn't accomplish anything for a dog. But they know so much more of the things that pertain to a dog's world that a man can feel humble in comparison.

We talk of dogs having an intuitive understanding; probably part of it is telepathic. But part of it is due to keen senses that convey sounds we can't hear and odors we can't smell.

If it came to a showdown and a man with nothing but his two hands had to eke out an existence from the country, he wouldn't make it; whereas a dog, under the same circumstances, would probably survive—and a dog has only his jaws. A man who had to crawl to within biting distance of his prey wouldn't stand the ghost of a chance.

Probably every really sympathetic dog owner who has learned to know and understand his dog and has had the experience of feeling particularly discouraged at some adversity of fate, who has been sitting disconsolately in a chair

The River Queen moored at Captain Salisbury's float.

feeling pretty blue and discouraged, has had the faithful dog interpret his mood well enough so that he arises softly from a reclining position, moves gently over and pushes a reassuring nose into his master's hand, giving a message of love and affection.

Some philosopher advised a young man to hitch his wagon to a star, but if a man will live his life so he can be really worthy of a good dog's affection, he doesn't need to look much farther for a worthwhile ambition.

CHAPTER THIRTEEN

Dance Hall Girls and Bandits

Indian summer was a warm benediction over the Delta country. Daylight saving time was a thing of the past. The nights were crisply cool, but the days were warm, and, for the most part, windless.

Dick DeShazer was building a new type of house cruiser, one which he had designed from his vast experience with boats, and it was in the final stages of construction at Isleton.

He wanted us to look it over, but it was rather prosaic to just drive up and back, so he suggested we take the River Queen, go through Taylor Slough, Piper Slough, False River, the San Joaquin River, through Threemile Slough into the Sacramento River; then up to a new restaurant he had heard a lot about at Rio Vista, have lunch there; then go on to the boat works at Isleton; then on up the Sacramento River to Walnut Grove, tie up there, and get a taxi to take us over to Giusti's. Then we could come back by Georgiana Slough in the moonlight.

There was about a three-quarter moon and the weather gave promise of remaining clear, so we decided to make the trip.

The new restaurant at the Rio Vista marina, called "The

Point," really lived up to its reputation. It had a menu with a wide variety of dishes and the dishes were good. It had cold wine ready to be served, and a dining room with a superb view of the marina and the river.

I am having trouble keeping up with these eating places along the river. There are too many of them, and they are too good.

There are perhaps a round dozen of these restaurants— some of them being rather large and ranking with the best eating places anywhere in the country; others, which are small family-type restaurants catering to yachtsmen and fishermen, are places where no one gives a hang what the customers are wearing just so they comply with the law. A person who has been fishing all day, cutting bait and baiting hooks, can come just as he is and be made to feel right at home.

I would like to cover all of these restaurants and give my firsthand experiences but, after all, this is a book about cruising; and we get in the habit of going to certain restaurants where the food is so nice that we just don't care to explore the new places.

And it is lot of downright fun to eat at a place where the proprietor is a friend, the waitresses are personal friends, and the whole atmosphere is that of an informal club of which the diner feels he is a charter member.

Such an atmosphere means more than food; but, when one can find that atmosphere *and* good food, the combination is irresistible.

We finished our inspection of Dick's boat at Isleton; and it is really some boat.

Forty-two feet long, with a beam in excess of fourteen feet, it is roomy, graceful, and durable. Actually, it is built like a battleship.

Dick spent probably an hour and a half pointing out little comforts which his experience had indicated would be convenient to the yachtsman, things which would suggest themselves only to someone who knew the yachting business from A to Z.

This boat is to be equipped with everything—air conditioning, a big electric refrigerator, a television, hot and cold running water, a spacious shower, full-sized double beds and twin beds, ample storage room, lots of drawer space—in short, everything that is needed for gracious living anywhere, all packed into forty-two feet of masterful efficiency.

Between the east bank of the Sacramento River at Walnut Grove and the west bank of the North Fork of the Mokelumne at Giusti's, there is a landlocked distance of approximately a mile, perhaps a little more.

We had been advised that there was a taxi service at Walnut Grove, and planned to leave our boat at the dock there and go over to Giusti's for cocktails and dinner.

We hadn't much more than left Isleton, however, when we saw a fishing boat with an outboard motor making its way toward us. And then we recognized Manuel Morais (the "Mo" of Giusti's) as one of the fishermen.

We tried to get him to come aboard and let us tow his outboard motor outfit up to Walnut Grove, but he felt he could make better time and he was scheduled to be there at six o'clock sharp; so we told him what we had in mind.

"Mo" listened gravely, told us he would be glad to see us, and then went speeding on up the river.

What happened is so indicative of "Mo" and of the spirit that permeates Giusti's that it is worth recounting.

When "Mo" got to Walnut Grove, he telephoned "Lo" at the bar at Giusti's and said in effect, "Gardner and a party are coming up to Walnut Grove. They don't have any transportation to get over to our place. They think there is a taxicab. They don't know there isn't any taxi service at Walnut Grove.

"They'll probably telephone you to tell you they've changed their plans. When they do, telephone me at Walnut

"Mo" of Giusti's comes aboard for a visit.

Grove and I'll pick them up and give them transportation down to our place; then we'll arrange with someone to take them back when they're ready to go to the boat."

And that was what happened. We telephoned "Lo" to tell him that we had had to change our plans. "Lo" simply laughed and said, " 'Mo' is waiting for a call. Just stay where you are and he'll pick you up."

So "Mo" picked us up and drove us down to Giusti's, where we had drinks and dinner in the delightful, friendly family atmosphere of the place; and then the young man, who goes by the name of "Dynamite," drove us back to the boat.

By this time, the evening was well along and the moonlight was all we had to rely on.

Dick DeShazer took over the piloting; and Dick has the eyes of a cat.

I stood up for a while looking out over his shoulder, trying to see where we were going, but I finally gave it up.

At that hour of the night, the water was a perfect mirror reflecting the levees, the dark masses of trees and brush along the banks, making it appear we were floating in the center of a little pool of illumination completely ringed with ominously dark obstacles and studded with star reflections.

But Dick's practiced eyes knew where the channel twisted, knew where an opening would appear just before it seemed we were due to run into that black border.

I was afraid of floating logs, but somehow Dick and Sam were able to spot any obstacles in our course; and, after a while, I decided I was in safe hands so I sat down and relaxed.

We got some music on the radio, turned on an electric heater which warmed up the cabin, and glided along through the reflecting waters until, finally, I found myself getting sleepy.

Despite the fact that I disliked to forgo any of the thrilling moments of moonlight cruising, I realized that I had had quite a strenuous day and that I am no longer as young as I once was.

So I surrendered gracefully, went back to the lower berth in the back, pulled a blanket over me, adjusted the pillow, opened the window so I could lie there looking at the banks of the slough gliding silently by, and promptly went to sleep.

I wakened when we were about half an hour out of our berth, came up front, joined the crowd again and watched the shores go by.

It had taken us a little less than three hours cruising at half speed to come down from Giusti's to Bethel Island. And just as we were docking, a bank of fog started moving in.

I shudder to think what would have happened if we had encountered that fog earlier in our journey. And then I thought of Captain Salisbury, who had spent years of his life tugboating on the Delta—not only navigating through dense fog, but towing a string of heavily loaded barges behind him.

As far as I am concerned, it would be bad enough to try to take a tugboat up in the river country on a clear night. A foggy night would be impossible. And then to think of having a string of five-thousand-ton barges coming along behind, ready to crush a tugboat like an eggshell, the experience becomes a potential nightmare.

There is romance in connection with the river, and people who have to do with boats somehow develop an individuality.

In the old river days, people had plenty of excitement, plenty of emergencies to cope with; and they had to be able to cope with those emergencies, to reach instantaneous decisions; and, for the most part, those decisions had to be right the first time. Men who made mistakes on the river didn't last very long.

Captain Quinn was telling us about an interesting holdup in the early days of river boating.

In those days, there was a little boat which made a daily run from Stockton to Isleton. In fact, transportation was largely by river and these cities along the river were serviced by boats which carried freight and passengers on a daily schedule.

The Isleton boat put in at a little harbor at Frank's Tract; and just as it was docking, a man stepped aboard, adjusted a mask, pointed a gun at the captain, and said, "Pull your boat away from the dock and over to that island."

The captain saw the steely eyes of the masked bandit and knew instinctively that the man meant business. He pulled his boat over to the island.

The bandit proceeded to rob the captain and the protesting passengers.

Then, another riverboat came down the channel and the bandit said to the captain, "Whistle that boat in over here."

The captain had to comply. He started playing tunes on the whistle and the other boat came over to see what was the matter.

It was at that moment, as the bandit was preparing to step

aboard the other boat, that the engineer, who had been watching his opportunity, tapped the bandit on the head with a metal bar.

The bandit fell overboard, bobbed to the surface, still carrying the gun in his right hand; then, treading water, promptly proceeded to shoot the captain of the incoming boat in the shoulder.

But the two boats were close together and the bandit was trapped between the two in the water. To be sure, he had a revolver, but he hadn't figured on the wrath of the irate passengers, who promptly proceeded to bombard him with every missile they could get hold of, ranging from baskets and suitcases to blankets hastily stripped from beds in the staterooms.

The bandit couldn't cope with all that barrage and was drowned there between the two boats.

It is interesting to note the changes which take place over a period of years. Nowadays it is doubtful if a passenger would throw his packed suitcase at a bandit.

Thinking back on the changes in rivers, I remember the old days on the Yukon River—on the heels of the gold rush.

When I knew the Yukon I was just a kid, but it was only six or seven years after the big discovery, and the whole Klondike was still in the grip of mining fever.

A railroad had been constructed from Skagway to White Horse; but the only means of reaching Dawson City was by boat, which went from White Horse down through Lake Laberge into the Yukon River, and so down to Dawson.

During the winter, an attempt was made to keep a stageline going; but this was precarious transportation, and only for the very hardy and the comparatively wealthy.

The river and the lakes would freeze during the winter, and the famous Lake Laberge was the last to go out. So river transportation from White Horse to Dawson really depended on when the ice became thin enough in Lake Laberge for the river steamers to go pushing through it.

Needless to say, the people who were jammed up at Skagway and at White Horse waiting for the first steamships to run presented a tremendous problem.

There were three classes of people who absolutely had to be on the first boats going from White Horse to Dawson City.

One class was the mining executives who had gone "outside" for the winter and had to get back to assume charge of their properties. These people and their wives had to be on the first boat.

But many of the lesser executives had stayed on the "inside" and had spent the long, dark winter in Dawson City, separated from their families. Their wives were to join them during the summer, and the big companies insisted that these wives have a high priority of transportation, so they were also on the first boats going to Dawson City.

The third class was equally important and, in those days, presented a very great problem. This third class was composed of the dance hall girls, who were going in to Dawson City dance halls. They also had a high priority—in fact, a very high priority indeed.

Now, in those days, the "good women" didn't mix with the "bad women."

In fact, it was a gesture for the good women to hold their voluminous skirts slightly up and to one side as they walked past one of the "painted hussies."

Actually, these dance hall girls were raving beauties. They were the cream of the crop. They had to have sufficient capital to transport themselves into the Klondike; they had to be sufficiently certain of themselves to know that they could make a profit on their investment during the relatively short summer season before they had to catch the last boat out just before Lake Laberge froze up again.

The problem was how you mixed these wives of the mining executives with the dance hall girls.

If the truth had been known by the wives, that boat would

have presented a difficult problem during the several days it took to get from White Horse to Dawson.

So the old-time miners in the community handled the problem with individuality, acumen, and judgment—just as they handled all other problems, which they took in their stride.

The word was passed that every dance hall girl coming in was to tell all the other passengers that she was the wife of a member of the Canadian Parliament, coming in to join her husband.

Human nature being what it is, many of the wives of the mining executives—finding themselves chatting vis-a-vis at the dining table with a beautiful young woman who was the wife of a member of the Canadian Parliament—would think that this could form the basis of a lasting friendship, at least one which would be advantageous during the long summer months in Dawson.

The old-timers were known as the "sourdoughs"; the newcomers, as the "cheechakos."

In due course, the boat would give a raucous blast on its whistle as it triumphantly steamed into its destination at Dawson. The wives would be gathered in the eager manly arms of the waiting executives and, after an interval, would tell their husbands about the very delightful wife of the member of the Canadian Parliament that they must "be nice to."

The husband would then disillusion his wife by initiating her into the secret of the Yukon.

By that time, the wife was enough of a veteran so that she was not only willing to ride along with the gag, but thought it rather amusing.

As far as I know, that secret was kept perfectly. No one ever blabbed.

I went down on the first boat through the ice on Lake Laberge, and it was crowded with the wives of executives and dance hall girls, and I saw these beautiful friendships

210

being formed and heard about the wives of the Canadian Parliament.

I know for a fact that there were quite a few people aboard the boat who knew all about the secret, but no one ever broke the unwritten law. The dance hall girls remained as the wives of the members of Parliament.

All of which is as it should be. And, again, we face the fact that we have lost a lot when we gave up our river transportation.

CHAPTER FOURTEEN

New Adventures And Old Friends

I kept my boats in use in the Delta until late in the fall of 1965. Then, in the early spring of 1966, we made another expedition to Baja California by means of four-wheel-drive automobiles, some of J. W. Black's specially designed "Grasshoppers," and helicopters. We had quite a few adventures on that trip, adventures which I related in a book entitled *Off the Beaten Track in Baja.**

Then with the yachting season of 1966 I found myself irresistibly drawn back to the Delta country.

I sold the thirty-two-foot Whit-Craft which I had, and bought a thirty-four-foot later model Whit-Craft as a companion boat to the River Queen.

This new Whit-Craft has an electric generator, an electric kitchen, a very nice shower with hot and cold running water, and a large refrigerator. It made an ideal second boat for our camping trips.

We visited with the DeShazers, and Dick and Moyne were as impatient to get out on another trip of camping and exploration as we were, but all of us were tied up with various and sundry odds and ends of business.

Some problems arose in connection with my books, and Helen King, the editor at William Morrow & Company who

* William Morrow & Company, Inc.; 1967.

212

Helen King contributes her share . . .

            . . . to the catch of catfish.

The Hon. Richard A. McGee, head of the entire California prison system . . .

. . . relaxes aboard the River Queen.

has been in charge of my manuscripts for some twenty-five years, decided to come out to California for a conference.

I asked her over the telephone whether she preferred to meet me at my ranch in Temecula or on the houseboats in the Delta, and, since she had edited *The World of Water*, her answer was instantaneous. She wanted to meet me on the Delta.

So, we picked up Helen King in San Francisco, took her out to the Delta, initiated her into the joys of catfishing and camping on a boat, took her down to see Captain Salisbury and Red, and, incidentally, had her wipe our eyes in catfishing.

The Honorable Richard A. McGee, the administrator of the entire penal system of California, wanted a conference and he, too, decided that it would be nice to have a conference on a house cruiser where we wouldn't be interrupted.

So, we met Dick McGee at the Stockton airport, whisked him out to the River Queen, took him up the river, and had a business conversation away from telephones, away from interruptions, and on the calm tranquillity of the Delta waters.

Then, the president of my publishing company, Larry Hughes, had a whole series of important problems which had to be discussed. Either he had to come to California or I had to go to New York.

Shamelessly I referred him to Helen King and the joys of conferring on a house cruiser, and, without any further argument, Larry and his wife, Rose, decided to fly to California to have our conferences on the River Queen.

Again we combined business with pleasure. We introduced them to "Chuckawalla Slim" and his wife, to Captain Salisbury and Red, to the DeShazers, and several other outstanding characters in the Delta country.

By this time, the Delta country was "home" to me. We were getting a whole string of friends all along the waterways. And it was a real pleasure to go and visit with these friends.

215

Again, I was surprised to find the extent to which my book, *The World of Water*, had been read and the influence it had had. Almost everywhere I went people would stop me, tell me that they recognized me from my pictures; that they had been intrigued by my description of the Delta, had come up and rented a houseboat and were having the time of their lives. They wanted to thank me in person for getting them acquainted with a wonderful country.

From time to time, the people in passing cruisers would wave in recognition and shout messages about my book, and,

L. to R.: Captain Salisbury, Larry Hughes, Sam Hicks, Rose Hughes, Jean Bethell lunching aboard the River Queen.

216

Larry Hughes listens to one of Captain Salisbury's tall tales.

L. to R.: Captain Salisbury, Jean Bethell, Larry Hughes, Sam Hicks.

Larry Hughes enjoys a magazine while Sam Hicks pilots the River Queen up one of the countless sloughs.

at times, our friends along the banks who had learned to recognize the house cruisers we had would feel offended if we were in a hurry and went on by without stopping.

And many of these friendships are very warm.

One Sunday morning we developed mechanical troubles. These were about the only mechanical troubles we had had and they came all at once in a whole series. Sam could cope with most of them, but we developed a motor trouble which had him stopped. We drifted into one of the islands and wondered what we were going to do next.

Of course, we had a radio so that it would have been possible to have called the Coast Guard for help, but I wanted to use that only as a last resort.

The people who live on the ranches do not take kindly, as a rule, to boatmen who are in trouble. In the first place, there are too many boatmen and, in the second place, most of the boatmen are too inconsiderate of the rights of the ranchers to

218

cause any rancher to want to go out of his way to help a boatman—and when one is in trouble in the island country it is indeed a long distance out of the way for a rancher to get help.

Then Sam realized that only a quarter of a mile or so away were our friends, the Fujimotos.

The Fujimotos are a wonderful Japanese family. We had made their acquaintance when we first started cruising the Delta, and, from time to time, we had entertained them aboard the River Queen.

So Sam went down to see if Hideo Fujimoto was home.

The results were beyond all expectations.

Mr. Fujimoto not only was home, but he had the true

We formed a warm friendship with the Fujimotos. L. to R.: The Author, Freeman (Doc) Lewis, Mrs. Hideo Fujimoto, and her husband.

friendship of the Oriental. He hunted up a man who is a positive genius with marine motors, and he and this man came up to our boat, lifted the hatches, descended down into the motors and, within a matter of minutes, diagnosed the trouble, made emergency repairs which would prevent a recurrence, and had things running like clockwork.

Some of my warmest friendships have been with the Japanese and the Chinese, and, in China, I have had people risk their very lives to accommodate me because they were my friends. In Japan I have been embarrassed at the extent to which my friends inconvenienced themselves in order to see that my every wish was fulfilled.

Now, in the Delta, my friendships were contributing to my weight problem.

I knew so many people, so many restaurant owners, that I wanted to eat out every night when we weren't out on the house cruisers, and dining out in the Delta can be a devastating experience to one who is inclined to put on weight.

Sam Hicks relaxes in the sun . . .

. . . until the fish strikes.

No matter how determined one may be that he is going to eat only a small amount, the fact remains that Alfred Wong's Chinese cooking at the Bel-Isle, the Mexican dishes at the restaurants in Brentwood, the incomparable food and service at the Riverview, and, above all, the repasts at Giusti's . . . well, I simply can't send such food back to the kitchen.

Sam is relatively young and has no weight problem. I usually make an agreement with him before we get to the restaurant. I will order something which he likes and then surreptitiously unload half to two-thirds of my plate on his, but, even so, when I get to the Delta I want to eat out, and when I eat, I eat.

Came the day, however, when finally we had our business obligations pretty well lined up and were free to go out for a ten-day trip.

Some of our group start out for a fishing expedition in the Smith Craft. L. to R.: Sam Hicks, Moyne DeShazer, Dick DeShazer, and J. W. Black.

Once again we were going to take two boats for living and another two boats for running errands and keeping in touch with the telephone.

We had the River Queen as headquarters, and we let the women know that this was to be their boat. They could have their own television, watch the programs they liked, go to bed when they liked, get up when they liked.

Sam Hicks, Dick DeShazer, and I were going to live on the Whit-Craft with our own television, our own radios, watch the programs *we* wanted, play penny ante as late as we wanted, go to bed when we darn pleased, get up in the morning and lounge around in pajamas, sitting at the table sipping coffee and eating doughnuts and coffee cake.

Women were allowed on our boat only at certain hours, and then for the sole purpose of using the refrigerator. It was understood that they were not welcome if they came with broom, mop, dust rag, or criticism.

We had the Valco twenty-three-foot aluminum cruiser which is a streak in the water, a smooth-running means of keeping in touch with the telephone, and, if it became necessary to make a rush trip back to headquarters, would be just about as fast as an automobile.

Then we had the Smith Craft, an eighteen-foot aluminum-alloy boat which is an ideal "workhorse." This is equipped with a Homelite four-cycle motor and is a general knock-around boat which we could use to haul supplies, gasoline, extra water as we needed it. We could also use it to bring in cakes of ice as we wanted them, and when I camp I want *lots* of ice.

Knowing that we would be somewhere in the vicinity of Giusti's, we decided to leave an automobile parked at Giusti's so we could have all the land transportation we needed.

The Valco aluminum cruiser is a streak in the water.

This is, of course, a deluxe arrangement, but I am a deluxe camper.

I don't think I have ever had more enjoyable experiences than when we had camped out in our house cruisers on earlier trips, and I wanted to duplicate these experiences.

As a matter of fact, we found ourselves in luck all the way. How lucky we were to be we didn't even dream.

It all started with a friend, whose name I can't mention lest he be importuned by too many people. This friend told us of a secret slough in the waterways where there was an island covered with huge shade trees, grassy slopes running to the banks, where it was possible to tie house cruisers right to the trees, where chairs could be spread out in the shade, where one could have all the pleasures of camping and living in house cruisers, and where the scenery was breathtaking in its beauty.

This spot, my friend declared, was known only to a few of his intimates, and, as a condition of going there, when people

Larry Hughes proudly displays his prize catch.

Rose Hughes lands a catfish in one of her secret fishing grounds.

asked us where we were camped, we must either become vague and change the subject or else give a purely fictitious location.

So, once again, we found ourselves engaged in all the anticipation which is so much a part of any good adventure.

We got together with the DeShazers for a couple of nights, went out to dinner, came back mellowed with food and good wine, relaxed in the DeShazer living room, looked at colored slides of previous trips, studied maps, and Jean and Moyne wrote out lists of supplies.

Then we started loading boats, which was quite a job, particularly in the case of the new boat.

A person living on a boat gradually accumulates a lot of material which he doesn't need to take ashore every time, spare clothes, flashlights, extra coats, fishing tackle, and all sorts of paraphernalia including kitchenware.

Starting with an absolutely brand-new boat which is completely empty of personal effects calls for a lot more effort than one would realize at first.

Each of our house cruisers had a kitchen and these kitchens each needed a complete supply of frying pans, coffee percolators, knives, forks, spoons, cups, saucers, and dishes. Then there were staple supplies of salt, pepper, sugar, tea, coffee, etc.

It might be mentioned in passing that while Sam Hicks and I usually take black-and-white photographs, Dick DeShazer and Jean Bethell take colored pictures, and recently, Moyne has joined the ranks of color enthusiasts.

The reason that Sam and I take black-and-white pictures is purely economical. In writing a book or a magazine article which is illustrated with photographs it is, of course, much more expensive to use color than black-and-white. Therefore, the editors want plenty of black-and-white photographs, not so many color shots.

On the other hand, when it comes to sitting around and reliving once more the memories of prior trips, or showing friends something new in the line of boating, colored photographs and a projector really tell the story.

So, on these nights when we sat around the DeShazers' living room, we almost always wound up by bringing out the projector, setting up the screen, and running through a new batch of pictures which had just come in, or bringing out one of the older reels so we could relive the experiences of some former trip.

In this book, since I am trying to tell something of the charm of relaxing in the waterways of the Delta, I would be remiss if I neglected to mention these joys of anticipation and preparation.

Because my problems are complex, my equipment has to

be complex. If I had been an ordinary vacationist the two DeShazers, Jean, Sam, and I could have simply boarded the River Queen and taken off on a carefree vacation, but since I had to be in touch with my office and in almost daily touch with a post office somewhere, I had to have a portable office with typewriters, stationery, dictating machines, and facilities for dashing back and forth without disrupting the entire camp—hence we took four boats, loaded with everything we could think of.

We made two trips as far as Giusti's. Jean and Moyne drove up in two automobiles while Sam, Dick, and I took the Smith Craft and the Valco up by the waterway route.

Arriving about the same time the automobiles did, we tied up our boats at the guest docks at Giusti's, had drinks at the bar and then a repast in the dining room.

After dinner we got in the second car Moyne had driven up,

We went to bed early without bothering to tighten our stern anchor on the River Queen.

went back to our house trailers, went to sleep, got up the next morning, put a few cakes of ice in our plastic iceboxes so we could have plenty of ice-cold drinks and watermelons without cluttering up the electric refrigerators, and were on our way.

We arrived at Giusti's, picked up the Smith Craft as a tow, and Moyne and Jean piloted the Valco. We went up to The Meadows, arriving there in due course, finding the place fairly well crowded, and so turned down into Snodgrass Slough where we found our old mooring places vacant and could tie up for the night.

We had an early dinner that night and briefly tested Moyne's portable color television set on the River Queen, finding that it worked perfectly. We went to bed early and slept in the blissful silence of the calm night.

The next day we started exploring. We left the two house cruisers, took the light, fast boats, and finally not only located the secret mooring place we had been told about, but found that it was everything we had hoped.

Jean Bethell and Moyne DeShazer spend a lazy summer afternoon on the forward deck of the River Queen.

We used our light, fast boats to explore.

So, we moved our house cruisers into this new place and established a permanent camp.

For a week we relaxed, having a hilarious penny ante game in which we played for matches; but since the matches were restricted to just so many to a customer, it became a real battle to see who could hang onto his lot.

We took photographs, we used our light, fast boats to explore new twists and turns in the waterways, we fished, we relaxed in the shade of the trees in comfortable chairs. We went swimming. From time to time we went for provisions, for telephoning, and for mail.

We renewed our acquaintance with our Chinese friends at Locke in the Yuen Chong Market.

The Valco and the Smith Craft, tied up between the two house cruisers.

I wrote about these people in my earlier book, *The World of Water*, but readers who are not familiar with that book should know more of these Chinese people and the market.

Years ago when I was exploring the Orient and getting a wealth of material for stories which had a Chinese background, I lived in a house in Canton with a family of Chinese friends. Unfortunately, the younger generation could speak English. The older people could talk only Chinese. I say it was unfortunate that the younger people could speak English, because they made a habit of addressing me in English and acting as interpreter for the older people.

On the other hand, when I was alone with the older people I had to resort to Cantonese.

And because during my early legal career I had specialized

230

in representing "Chinatown" I had at one time a fair knowledge of Cantonese. I greatly regret that many, many years of disuse has caused me to forget much of what I knew.

My first meeting with the Chinese at Locke had been in 1964 when Sam and I went into the market and met George Marr who has charge of the meat department.

I started talking Chinese to George Marr, using some of the poetic Chinese which is so intriguing.

For instance, when one Chinese meets another he will be very apt to say, *"Hoh shai kai mah?"*

This is a question which literally translated means, "Is the whole world good?"

The Chinese will gravely answer, *"Hoh shai kai,"* meaning the whole world is good.

It is to be noted parenthetically that the *"mah"* is a question mark. Since the Cantonese langauge is a language of monosyllables and since there aren't enough monosyllables to go around, the Chinese have developed eight tones—actually from a technical standpoint there are nine tones—but there are eight principal tones. Each tone gives the word a different meaning. Under those circumstances it is impossible to indicate a question by a rising inflection of the voice at the end of the sentence. Therefore, the Chinese use a verbal question mark. It is, of course, this tonal value which gives the Chinese language its peculiar singsong effect. Very few people who hear a Chinese speaking, however, realize that each little singsong note gives each word its different meaning.

In any event, I talked a little Chinese with George Marr, who was busy cutting steaks to our specifications.

As Marr cut, I talked, and Marr began to show considerable interest.

At the end, when he had our steaks all cut and ready to wrap up, he hestitated, then reached in, took out one of the steaks, tossed it to one side, and cut another one to take its place.

231

He looked at me gravely and said, "Cannot sell bum steak to person who speaks good Chinese."

The grocery department is operated by Constance King and her brother-in-law, Stanford King.

Constance King, or "Connie," as she is generally known, is a remarkably beautiful Chinese. Because her husband works at a daytime job he can't be present at the store. Connie has a delightful, gentle personality and everyone who knows her loves her.

Stanford King has a droll sense of humor. He is something of a Chinese Will Rogers, and these three people have become our friends. It is a pleasure to see them whenever we go back to the Delta country.

Many people who come up to rent a houseboat make the mistake of buying too great a percentage of their provisions outside the Delta. It would give them a lot more fun to buy at the various really good stores in the Delta country where they could get acquainted with the merchants.

Vacationists would get a lot of fun buying as much as possible from the Yuen Chong Market in Locke, the Big Store in Walnut Grove, and the two markets at Bethel Island.

Locke and Walnut Grove are two old, old settlements along the river which have changed but little in the last hundred years.

These were Chinese settlements, and the whole architecture is reminiscent of the Chinatowns of years ago, the narrow streets, the buildings with residences on top and stores underneath, the hard benches on each side of the doors of some of the buildings.

Those benches undoubtedly go back to a time when the cities were running "wide open."

In those days, the hard, uncomfortable benches were occupied by Chinese who apparently were doing nothing except sitting there, but, actually, these Chinese knew just about every law officer and every detective in the district. When one

Constance King.

showed up, there would be a singsong chatter of Cantonese and the word would spread up and down the street like wildfire.

I remember one time walking down the streets of Chinatown in Los Angeles with a Chinese friend.

As is customary in Chinatown, we walked in single file, my friend ahead, I, a couple of steps behind. For a moment my friend forgot that I wasn't Chinese. We passed an innocent-looking tourist with a camera. My friend never turned his head in the slightest, kept right on with his shuffling walk, but called back over his shoulder, *"Ah peck yen ahm cha."*

In a house cruiser one has the placid river, the overhanging trees, and the stars.

From this I learned that the innocent-appearing tourist, gawking around with a camera, was actually a detective looking for opium smoking.

Doubtless, the detective thought that his "disguise" was perfect, that he could blunder into various places and ask fool questions. I wonder how he would have felt if he had known that, from time to time, as he passed places, Chinese without even turning their heads and not seeming to look at him would chant the words, *"Ah peck yen ahm cha."*

River-cruiser camping is different from any type of camping I have ever known. It is as if one had a small compact luxurious apartment which he could transfer on a magic carpet to any place he wanted, to place it under spreading shade trees and live a life of luxury.

Living in a well-appointed house trailer is somewhat similar; but in a house trailer that has electricity, waste disposal, and all the conveniences, one has to be in a trailer park. While some of these trailer parks are delightful places, there are neighbors to be considered.

234

In a house cruiser one doesn't have neighbors. One has the placid river, the overhanging trees, and the stars. And in a couple of house cruisers one can have the guests he wants. J. W. Black of Paradise, California, and his wife, Lois, came to visit us over a weekend. J. W. Black is a mechanical genius who has specialized in off-the-trail transportation, and Lois is an ardent angler.

We sat up as late as we liked and laughed as loud and as often as we wanted. We kept our TV sets on until all hours if we wished. Or, if the spirit moved us, we were in bed early, surrounded by the silence of the countryside.

It is surprising how entertaining penny ante can be when one is playing with a determination to hold onto as many of his matches as possible and get as many of the other fellow's matches as he can win. The game, of course, being spiced with conversational bait tending to make the other players think that you have them bigger than a house when you are

Lois Black, an ardent angler.

bluffing, or to make them think that you are bluffing when you have them bigger than a house.

And because the stakes are so infinitesimal as to be meaningless from an economic standpoint, the game can, at times, become really hilarious.

Then we would close up the game, sit for a half an hour or so sipping a hot drink, roll into bed, shut off the generator, and sink into the oblivion of peaceful slumber.

In the morning, we would start the generator, turn on the heat under the coffee percolator, turn on the radio and listen to our favorite commentator.

Bill Bates of the KTRB Modesto radio station is a salty character who is entirely different from any other radio announcer I know.

Bates has a regular program in which he chats with his listeners, interspersing comments with information about his personal health, the weather, and about oustanding events in the news.

He has been broadcasting for years and years, carrying on his distinctive brand of informal conversation so utterly different from the conventional pattern followed by radio reporters it is a pleasure to listen to him.

Bates must have a terrific following, and must deliver results for his clients because we have noticed over the years that he seems to keep the same sponsors for his program.

He comes on over the Modesto radio station at 8:15 in the morning, chats until Ralph King from Echo Summit in the Sierra Nevada Mountains comes on with a report on mountain weather. Then they talk back and forth about almost anything in the world.

Ralph, building a fire with an old newspaper, will find an article that interests him, and he and Bill will chat for two or three minutes about that article.

This is such a distinctly human trait that I think it appeals to listeners everywhere.

236

How many of us, building a fire with an old newspaper, have suddenly had our attention captured by some article and then sat there by the stove shivering in the cold, absorbed in an article in a paper which has long since been thrown away?

At 8:30 or thereabout, Bates gives way for a conventional news program, then comes on again at 8:45 when he will give additional weather information, pick up the telephone and chat with a furniture dealer who has the name of Vrh—pronounced Vurr—who is one of his sponsors, giving information about articles of furniture which are specials for the day, the two engaging in a considerable amount of badinage back and forth.

Bates handles his commercials in such a way that the listeners soon begin to feel that they know the sponsors as individuals.

He never leaves his audience behind but takes his listeners right along with him. He'll say, "Let's go down and see Johnny Pflocks"; and then he'll go on in a conversational tone to tell you about Johnny Pflocks and the tire retreading business—how long Pflocks has been in it, how he retreads the tires for the big trucks, the fact that truck owners have to retread tires not only once, but several times—and Johnny Pflocks is the boy who can do it. And, of course, persons driving passenger cars can get the benfit of all that experience.

Then Bates will give the time. And when Bates gives the time, he gives the *exact* time. Too many radio stations give the approximate time. Set your watch by the time they give and, an hour or two later, they'll give a time which is a minute off from the time given earlier. Not so with Bill Bates; he gives the time to the second.

Then Bates will say, "Now, let's go down and see Johnny Willinger at the Willinger Automotive Service. They're experts on speedometers, you know. If you have anything wrong with your speedometer, go to Johnny Willinger. I don't mean if something's wrong with your speedometer cable, I mean if

237

something is wrong with your speedometer. Everybody knows Johnny Willinger. The little bald-headed guy. He's been around for years. Now, he's got a son coming on in the business, going in with Johnny."

As far as I am concerned, this is the type of commercial I can listen to and feel that I'm actually meeting the people mentioned.

Not only does Bates give the exact time so you can set your watch to the second, but he gives complete data on the weather—particularly the velocity of the wind in the Delta.

During the summer months, the velocity of wind in the Delta is important to the people in the San Joaquin Valley because the wind which is funneled in from the ocean has a cooling effect; and if there's to be a twenty-five-mile west wind in the afternoon, the people around Modesto can count on a lower temperature.

As far as yachtsmen are concerned, knowing what the wind is going to be in the Delta is very much worthwhile. A ten-mile breeze is nothing; but a twenty-five-mile wind blowing against a tide can kick up a very nasty little chop, and presents a difficult problem when it comes to berthing a boat in one of the stalls in the marinas.

I suppose Bill Bates' audience in the Delta doesn't count with KTRB's station rating—but because of listening to Bates, I found myself switching to Rainbow bread in the market; and if I had a difficult retreading job, I feel I would drive the fifty-odd miles to let Johnny Pflocks work on it.

We got the habit of listening to Bill Bates in the Delta some years ago because of the forecast on winds in the Delta and, after a while, the listening became a habit; and, now, we're really old friends with Bates. We like to tune him in over our morning coffee.

I know full well that because of my peculiar problems I have to have equipment which I would not have if it weren't for those problems, and equipment which the average boatsman will not have.

238

Otherwise, I wouldn't travel in such a deluxe manner, but, on the other hand, I couldn't spend nearly as much money as I do in Delta travel. In order to make the money which finances that travel I have to spend a great deal.

This was brought home to me when, on one of our trips to Walnut Grove, we received information on the telephone which made it vital for us to communicate with camp and go back to camp with the information and return to the telephone, then back to camp again. This consumed altogether too much time and wasted a day of perfect vacation.

So, I decided to have Citizen's Band radio outfits installed on all the boats.

We already had walkie-talkies which were capable of communication over a mile or two, but couldn't be counted on to communicate over a distance of eight, ten or fifteen miles.

We had, of course, communications on the boats so that we could call out anywhere in the event of an emergency, but since the marine operators are exceedingly busy and the channels clogged with calls during weekends and vacation periods, we decided to try Citizen's Band radios on our next trip and see what could be accomplished with them.

We were fortunate in that we had perfect weather during the ten days we were camped, and the days were so enjoyable that they fairly whizzed past us on the calendar.

Then, it came time to go back and meet some important people who were coming to the ranch, get caught up on some business decisions, and put in a good many hours of uninterrupted dictation on business and correspondence.

I arranged with Dick when I left to get in touch with the best electronics man he could find and install Citizen's Band radios on the boats, and promised to be back in the early fall for another trip when we could test out some of the new gadgets we are putting on the boats as well as the Citizen's Band radios.

When some person with a houseboat or a cruiser finds a good place to tie up and enjoy life or a good catfishing spot, he guards the information carefully. When a fisherman finds a good eddy where there are plenty of cooperative catfish he throws a veil of secrecy about the location.

Of course, such places as The Meadows and Snodgrass Slough are well known and, in fact, the state is now in the process of making The Meadows and Snodgrass Slough into a state park.

This is a really beautiful part of the Delta country, uninhabited islands bordered with huge trees, the waters fairly well sheltered, the scenery a yachtsman's delight, and there are many places to tie up boats in the midst of that scenery.

The owners of the land have not objected to campers who are at all considerate and who leave clean camps, and this is the big thing.

It is to be remembered that all the land along the Delta tributaries is privately owned and while the water itself is tidewater and navigable and, therefore, open to the public, the minute a person puts a foot ashore he is trespassing.

In the proposed state park in The Meadows the state is planning to acquire enough of a strip of land so that there can be regular camps. In the other parts of the Delta country, yachtsmen have, from time to time, acquired land so that they can form yacht clubs and have their own places to camp. In other places yachtsmen have become friendly with the owners of the land so that the owner will give camping permission to one or two boat owners who have proven that they can leave clean camps, who will not break down fences, leave gates open, throw tin cans all over the place, or commit any of the thousand and one depredations which are, unfortunately, so prevalent wherever large numbers of vacationers make their camps.

It is not much of a job to leave a clean camp. A person needs a shovel to dig a deep hole for garbage and that is about all. And, if he doesn't have permission to dig a hole, he can have a big garbage can, which, when full, can be taken to one of the places where there is a garbage disposal unit.

240

Water skiing makes huge waves.

It is surprising, however, how many people disregard this first rule of camping and simply toss their tin cans either overboard or into the wild blackberry vines, or, at times, just simply leave them where they lie, and then go away.

With the vast increase in houseboat and cruiser rentals in the Delta region, this problem of garbage disposal is apt to become quite acute, and yachtsmen everywhere should unite to formulate a system of simple rules which will bring about a better understanding and better relations between the boat operators and the owners of property bordering the waterways.

One of the big problems is that posed by the water skier.

The expert skier wants plenty of thrills and lots of action. In order to get this he needs a very fast boat and he wants to cross back and forth across the wake of his own boat and other boats, using the waves of the wake as a springboard to

241

Kenneth Brown makes a high jump.

give him a chance to jump in the air or exercise his skill as a skier.

The trouble with this type of water skiing is that it makes huge waves and each of these waves tends to wash away an infinitesimal part of the levee. Over the months, thousands of these waves produce an undermining of the levee which is a cause of some concern to the property owners.

Also water skiers going past fishing boats or house cruisers quite frequently leave waves which are disastrous, rocking the boat to such an extent that dinner which is cooking on the boat's stove falls off to the floor.

Water skiers are aware of this and are generally trying to find places to ski where houseboats and cruisers are not moored, and houseboats try to find places free from water skiers.

242

For instance, in The Meadows it is an unwritten law that there is to be no skiing, whereas in adjoining Snodgrass Slough it is understood that water skiers have generally the right-of-way. So, anyone who moors a house cruiser in Snod-grass Slough should be aware that there will be water skiers from time to time and waves which will rock the boat.

Snodgrass Slough is quite wide and, if a person moors his boat so either the bow or stern is facing the bank, the waves are not particularly damaging. In the event a boat is moored parallel with the bank, however, the waves can cause a great deal of damage.

It is my feeling that even with the huge number of boats that are privately owned in the Delta region, the waterways have only begun to come into their own.

A vacation by boat is a wonderful vacation for the person who is renting, and the person who lives near enough to the waterways so he can use a boat over weekends will find that a boat is a very fine investment in recreation.

Lazy days in The Meadows.

Bud Remsburg's covered boat berths.

In the first place, boating is a family pastime. Just driving a boat is a lot of fun. The waterways are usually cool with at least a breeze stirring and sometimes a good brisk wind.

The average businessman who can get away Friday night and have Saturday and Sunday for recreation can go to the golf course if he is a golfer, but if he is not a golfer or is so attached to his family that he wants to take the family with him, there is absolutely nothing that I know of that can compare with life on a boat.

And since the hull of the boat is in cool water, the deck of the boat is usually reasonably cool.

Take, for instance, Bud Remsburg's Marina where we keep our boats. These berths are covered so that they are perpetually shaded. The cool water is on the hull of the boat. There is running water and electricity on the dock. There are garbage cans, clean spacious toilets and showers for both men and women, and the whole place is kept up so it is scrupulously clean.

As a result we find that many people will drive up from San Jose, San Francisco, or the other Bay Cities, park their cars in the big parking space which Remsburg keeps available, carry provisions down to their cruisers, connect up the electricity, and spend the weekend on the cruiser without ever even starting the boat motors.

They can sit out on deck and look over the waterway with the boats going back and forth. They can visit with congenial people who are also spending the weekend in boats. They can be cool where the outside country is baking in hot sunlight— and it is a natural coolness, not the artificial coolness of air conditioning.

These people have every housekeeping convenience at their fingertips, have a weekend of perfect relaxation, and return home refreshed. Their weekend vacation hasn't cost them a dime except for a little gasoline and hasn't been all spent in bumper-to-bumper traffic.

And there is no motel room which can match the conveniences of a houseboat or a well-appointed cruiser. A boat is, of course, far more compact. People are forced to get off the boat if they want to walk around very much, but for a person

Next in line for launching.

who wants to sit and read the Sunday papers, listen to the radio, watch television, doze and relax, the boat represents an ideal way to spend the weekend, and the Delta country is only a little over an hour's drive from the big cities of the bay area.

Considering all these advantages, it is a wonder that there aren't more boats than there are.

There are always good boats available for a little more than the price of a good automobile, and if a person wants to get a used boat from a reputable dealer and is willing to take good care of it, he can find the depreciation is remarkably low. If he wants to sell it, he can come very close to getting his money out of it.

Of course, if one buys a new boat, it is like anything else. There is a greater depreciation. However, the Whit-Craft, which I bought new and used for a couple of years and then sold, brought within a few hundred dollars of what I had paid for it in the first place, and, in the meantime, I had had all the fun of use and ownership.

Boat and trailer, hooked to a wire rope at the top of the incline.

When the boat is in the water, the trailer is returned for the
next load.

247

CHAPTER FIFTEEN

Indian Summer Days

We went back to the Delta during the latter part of October with some trepidation. It was getting pretty late in the season to go out for a two-week camping cruise.

However, there is an Indian summer in the Delta when the weather can be absolutely ideal, and there was some indication that we were going to have Indian summer weather for at least a few days.

So, the DeShazers, Jean, Sam, and I took the Valco Express Cruiser, the Smith Craft, the Whit-Craft, and the River Queen and once more started up the river.

The night before, we had driven an automobile up and parked it at Giusti's so that after we had made camp we could get into Giusti's in one of the light, fast boats, pick up the automobile, go to Locke or Walnut Grove—or, if necessary, to Rio Vista, or even to Antioch.

We expected we would have three or four days of calm, sunny weather while we were getting settled, then we anticipated some rain and perhaps some high wind. But aside from the fact that we would have a problem of tracking mud into the boats in the event of a rain, the weather wouldn't bother us too much until it became time to return. And when we started back, we intended to pick good weather.

It is no fun to be caught in a fog in the Delta country when one is trying to keep four boats together. In fact, it is no fun to be caught in a fog in the Delta country, period.

It can also get quite rough in the San Joaquin deepwater channel and in the expansive water at Frank's Tract if there is a high wind.

A house cruiser is a very seaworthy boat but, with its high sides, it presents quite a target for a heavy wind blowing across the beam.

On this trip, we had our new Citizen's Band radios installed.

These so-called Citizen's Band radios are a boon to the fleet owner who wants to keep in touch with his various units.

As has been mentioned, Leisure Landing has Citizen's Band radio units in its various boats and receives calls from all over the Delta.

As is always the case, I was in a hurry, and there was very

Morais and his wife come for a barbecue dinner aboard the River Queen. L. to R.: Dick DeShazer, Jean Bethell, "Mo," Moyne De-Shazer, Dolores Morais, Mark Morais, and the Author.

little time for adjusting and testing. As we found out after our return, a few days more of testing and checking the installation would have given us a great deal more efficiency.

We had a unit in Dick DeShazer's office, one in our trailers, a unit in each of the boats, and a unit in the automobile which we left up at Giusti's.

In this way, we could keep in touch with each other not only while we were cruising, but after we had made camp.

These radios certainly do a job.

When three or four boats are strung out over a mile or a mile and a half of water, it is very convenient to be able to pick up the microphone and pass instructions back and forth as easily as though we were still sitting in the same room.

There are times, however, when it is difficult to remember that the voices are going out over the air—particularly when one is tempted to make a wisecrack.

When we returned from base camp, we towed the Smith

On weekends, the guest dock at Giusti's may well be comfortably filled.

Our boats strung out.

Craft behind the River Queen; Moyne and Jean operated the Valco, and Dick came along in the Whit-Craft.

I wanted some coffee and had no difficulty in finding the coffee, but when the coffee was made, I looked high and low on that River Queen and couldn't find the chemical sweetener.

For the moment, I had forgotten about the radio.

Then I remembered, picked up the radio, and said, "River Queen calling Valco—come in, please." Instantly, Jean's voice said, "What do you want?"

"Where in heck do you girls keep your artificial sweetener?" I asked. "I've looked the place over and can't find it."

Jean said, "The tablets are in a little jar in the cupboard over the stove and to the left. There's no label on the jar."

So I ransacked the cabinet over the stove to the left, and finally came on a jar containing white tablets which had been stuffed at the top with cotton.

It seems that Jean and Moyne do not use artificial sweetener, but they had taken the tablets out of the bottle in which they came and placed them in a smaller jar.

Why women do this has never been determined.

They will invariably cook up a big pot of rice, eat part of it, put everything that is left in a smaller pot, and have the big pot to wash. Then they will eat part of the smaller pot, put the residue into a still smaller pot, and have the medium-sized pot to wash. Then they will eat a little rice, dump the residue out of the small pot into a bowl, have the small pot to wash; and if there should be a few teaspoonfuls of rice left, put that in a cup so they can wash the bowl.

When the going is good, a woman can get about five or six dish washings out of a pot of rice, or stew, or what have you.

Now, artificial sweetener tends to absorb moisture from the atmosphere so that, when it is shipped in containers, a little package which dehydrates the atmosphere in the jar is included with the pellets.

In transferring this particular bunch of pellets from the jar in which they came to the smaller jar packed with cotton, the girls had neglected to include the dehydrating package, and the pellets had crumpled into a soggy mass.

I made a few explosive remarks which, fortunately, were not heard on the air. Then over the radio came Jean's dulcet voice, "Did you find the sweetener all right?"

For the moment, I forgot that I had probably a wide audience and said, "Gosh, Jean, I put three of those tablets in the coffee. It tasted funny and I wondered if I had the right ones, so I took a couple of the tablets that were left out and looked at them under a magnifying glass. They were stamped 'Calomel'."

Jean, who knows my particular brand of humor through years of association, made no comment. Not so the half a hundred possessors of Citizen's Band radios who were tuned in along the line of travel.

252

These Citizen's Band radios have become big industry. The various four-wheel-drive automobile clubs are equipped with them, and there have been some very interesting developments as a result.

Once, when a detachment from the Sareea Al Jamel Club got up at the very summit of one of California's high mountains and rather foolishly started down the sheer mountainside, dodging big granite boulders and huge pine trees, they finally came to an impasse just about dark where they couldn't back up and there was a sheer drop of over a hundred feet ahead of them.

They tuned in a Citizen's Band radio, asking if any other members were listening,and promptly got a response from a distance of some thirty-five miles.

They explained their predicament. A cold night was coming on in the mountains; they were without food, water, or blankets; they were going to leave the cars where they were and hike down the side of the mountain in the dusk until they reached a camping place on a road a couple of miles below.

The Citizen's Band radios started working, and shortly after the stranded motorists got to the road and built a campfire, they saw headlights approaching; and other club members, together with members of the Chuckawalla Jeep Club, poured in with meat, barbecue grates, big coffeepots, sleeping bags, and a wealth of verbal ribbing.

A good time was had by all, and the night was one to be long remembered.

One time when J. W. Black was up in the high mountains back of Paradise and a part went out on one of the cars, his companion got on a Citizen's Band radio and found a man who could hear him down at Yuba City—a distance of some fifty miles.

He asked this operator to telephone collect to a relative in Paradise to obtain a new part for the car and bring it up to the place where they were stranded.

A few hours later, up came the relative with the part for the car.

Nowadays, what with walkie-talkies and Citizen's Band radios, it seems that just about everyone is talking.

Once when we were in camp on the River Queen, we tuned the set in and heard an operator in Riverside; then we heard another operator talking with a man in Oklahoma.

Those Citizen's Band radios are supposed to carry over only a short distance—some twenty to thirty miles—but when atmospheric conditions are right, they can indeed be heard over a long distance.

When we were adventuring in Mexico with airplanes and automobiles, we carried so-called walkie-talkies which are supposed to have a very limited range, but which were wonderful for carrying on conversations between the airplanes and the cars on the ground.

Yet we found that, quite frequently, conversations from people in Texas came in on those little hand-held walkie-talkies as plain as though the speakers were standing alongside shoulder-to-shoulder.

Before we had those walkie-talkies, we certainly had a job communicating. I would tie a note to a weight, open the airplane door a crack and, just as we flew over the cars, throw the rock down—hoping that the wind would not blow it back against the tail assembly of the airplane.

Now it should be a simple matter for people on the ground to read a note and give an affirmative or negative signal; but, when you are up in the air, it is difficult to see whether people below are nodding their heads or shaking them and, when they resorted to hand signals, it is surprising the amount of ambiguity which can be compressed into a brief space of time. And while you can toss a note from an airplane to the ground, there is no way of getting a communication back up to the airplane.

These walkie-talkies solved the problem wonderfully well.

254

And, of course, we used the walkie-talkies up in the Delta in connection with the Citizen's Band radio communication on the boat. By tuning to the same wave band as that of the walkie-talkie, we could converse over relatively short distances with the greatest of ease.

Freeman Lewis—Vice-President in charge of sales at Simon & Schuster and Pocket Books, and known throughout the book trade as "Doc" Lewis—is one of the shrewdest sales executives in the business. We were due to have a conference and, since he knew we were out in the Delta country, "Doc" decided that he would like to join us in camp.

So it was arranged that he would fly to San Francisco, pick up a rent-car there, and drive to Giusti's where we would meet him with a boat at a specified time.

"Doc" is quite a yachting enthusiast, although he prefers sail to power. He has a small sailboat which he keeps in Long Island Sound and, on weekends whenever he can get away, goes out for a two- or three-hour sail.

Since this boat has no power of any kind, it is sometimes

Freeman (Doc) Lewis comes to the bow of the Whit-Craft.

rather tricky to navigate in picking up a mooring or threading one's way through heavy traffic.

"Doc" loves it.

When we went in to Giusti's to pick him up, we were trying to travel on a schedule and were reminded how rapidly times can change.

Since the last time we were up the Mokelumne River, the salmon had started running and, now, the eight or ten miles of river which we had to traverse was swarming with boats—the fishermen trolling for salmon.

Personally, I am not a salmon fisherman. I go for catfish with barbless hooks.

Therefore, I have to take what I can learn about salmon fishing from the word of experts.

Two of those experts I know, "senior citizens" so-called, are a brother and sister, Finley McRae and Flora Gene Carberry.

Mr. & Mrs. Sheldon Perry even take their dog fishing.

Salmon fishermen trolling the Mokelumne River.

From day to day, these two would come trolling past our boats and almost invariably they had fish—good-sized black bass and salmon. They used the same equipment as other fishermen, they trolled at the same speed that the others did, but somehow they always managed to have lots of fish while others trolled either fruitlessly or with mediocre success.

Eventually, we got acquainted with McRae and his sister; and they told Sam that when the salmon run up the river they are not eating, will not bite on bait, and do not grab at a trolling spinner because they think it is something to eat, but because they are angry and lash out at anything that gets in their way.

Therefore, McRae says, you troll along close to the bottom

257

Our friends and neighbors, Finley McRae and his sister, Mrs. Flora Gene Carberry, show us a couple of salmon they have just caught.

at just the right speed, with just the right weight on your line, and sooner or later a salmon will savagely attack the flashing lure and find himself hooked.

Mrs. Carberry, McRae's sister, is the real fisherman in the crowd. Everyone admits that she is the champion on the river. Something about the way she handles a fishing rod or something about the way she holds her mouth gets results.

We were the recipients of one of the salmon she had caught —a seven- or eight-pound beauty, and it was a wonderful delicacy.

However, all these fishing boats certainly raised hob with any kind of schedule when it came to traveling back and forth to Giusti's.

As we've said, it is etiquette to slow down when you meet a

boat; and whenever you pass a trolling boat, one should move over close to the bank to stay clear of the lines, and reduce speed to such a point that you fairly crawl past the trolling fishermen.

Our time from camp on the Mokelumne River to Giusti's was just about trebled because of this vast fleet of fishing boats. And when we went in to pick up "Doc" Lewis, despite the fact we had made ample allowance for fishing boats, we ran into an emergency which caused at least a twenty-minute delay.

We rounded a bend in the river and came to a point where the boats were all clustered together watching another boat about two hundred yards away, where a fisherman was battling a huge fish.

This fisherman had very light tackle and the fish, apparently, was a huge one. The boatman had been playing the fish for some thirty-five minutes when we arrived and, because the fish was so big and the man's tackle so light, the fish was

This fisherman is playing a huge striped bass.

pretty much in charge of the situation—making runs whenever he felt like it. Slowly but surely, he was getting tired, but he could still take the line just about any place he wished.

Therefore, other fishermen were giving the angler the whole river so that the fishing line wouldn't get tangled in their propellers.

After about fifteen minutes, the fish got close to the other shore so that we were able to sneak by and be on our way.

It wasn't until later on that we found out what had happened to the fish. It was a huge striped bass, originally reported as being over thirty pounds in weight. However, it turned out to be in the twenties when it was finally weighed.

The angler fought that fish for some forty-five minutes and then had his reel break. Another boat streaked up to the tackle store at New Hope Landing and the tackle man came out with a new pole, line, and reel. After a lot of debate, they reeled off about twenty feet of slack back of the tension point on the line, the dealer cut the line at the end of the slack, made a swift knot tying the new line to the new pole and reel. And, fortunately for the angler, the operation was completed before the big fish took another run.

After that, the angler was more in command of the situation and, eventually, landed the fish.

At Giusti's, "Doc" Lewis arrived right on the second, which was remarkable since he had flown to San Francisco, then picked up a rent-car, driven over strange roads to the Delta region, then followed a map which we had made for him—arriving at Giusti's without any trouble.

We parked "Doc's" rented car and took him up to camp in the Valco cruiser, barely crawling along, explaining to him en route that we had found our favorite camp preempted by other cruisers so we had had to find a new camping spot. But we had one which gave us a reasonable amount of shade, a chance to put out chairs under the trees, and gave us a good place to tie up.

260

Wick Daly and Kent Koser with striped bass, some over 20 lbs.

"Doc" was inclined to brag about his accomplishments in playing bridge or gin rummy; but he claimed to be an absolute neophyte, a complete babe in the woods when it came to penny ante.

As subsequent events turned out, he was an expert at any game we wanted to call; and we had invented one game which it was certain "Doc" Lewis could never have heard of before.

It is our own invention; it is just about the wildest game I know of, and it makes for the most fun.

Any card player will get hysterics at simply listening to a description of the game but, when it is actually played, it turns out to be a very scientific game with lots of action.

The trouble with orthodox penny ante when only three people are playing—and Dick, Sam, and I play often—is that the game becomes so slow that the only possible way to speed it up is to try to bluff, and it wasn't unusual for all three of us to be bluffing at the same time. Moreover, when one player draws to a four-card flush and makes it, the other two players are apt not even to have a pair. Under such circumstances the game is inclined to get monotonous.

However, with our new game, there is always so much action and so much speed that three people can play it successfully.

We start out with a full deck and *two* jokers—both jokers are wild.

There are four nines in the deck, and all four nines are wild.

There are four threes in the deck, and any person who has a three can trade it in at *any* time for a different card. He has the option of either keeping the three or trading it in.

This makes a game which would speedily get out of hand when one remembers that it is a modification of the card game known as "Seven-Toed Pete"—that is, there are two hole cards, four cards face up, and one card down, and the player plays the five best cards in his hand, betting on each card as in stud.

The scientific part of our game is that whenever any player gets three wild cards in his hand at *any* time, he has to turn over his cards, loses his interest in the pot, and is out of the game.

It is not unusual for a person to get two wild cards early in the game—sometimes both face up, sometimes one or perhaps both down. Usually the other players sense when the opposing player has a hand of this sort and, of course, if the two wild cards are face up, they know it.

The players, therefore, bet not only on the strength of their own hands, but on the chance that—with six wild cards in the deck—the opposing player will draw a third wild card and hence lose all interest in the pot.

The opposing player, on the other hand, tries to make the stakes high enough so the opposition will not care to continue, and so he can win without the risk of drawing the third wild card.

Since the game is played as stud poker is played, with a bet on every card and then a bet on the final hand, it is a very rapid game full of action and conversation.

If, for instance, a player has one wild card and a three showing and *doesn't* trade in the three, it is a pretty good indication that he has another wild card in the hole and doesn't dare to trade the three in for fear that, in doing so, he will pick up his third wild card which will disqualify him and forfeit his entire interest in the pot.

Therefore, a shrewd player can bluff with a three. If he has a three up which he doesn't trade, the other players are quick to assume that he already has two wild cards.

This game never gets slow or static; it is always a wild-eyed game with lots of action.

Life was a beautiful idyll of existence, getting away from all the noise and rush, sleeping as late as we pleased, going to bed whenever we wanted to, taking photographs, exploring in the small boats, having jam sessions on the houseboats.

Because Pocket Books have published my paperbacked editions for years—having sold well over a hundred million copies—"Doc" Lewis and I had a reasonable amount of business to discuss. But it was more fun having fun than discussing business, so our business talks were masterpieces of monosyllabic brevity. I would listen for ten or fifteen seconds to the

Dick DeShazer, watching the Smith Craft, which has broken from its moorings and is drifting into dangerously shallow waters.

first sentence and halfway through the second sentence. Then I'd interrupt to say, "Okay, Doc, do whatever you think is best. You've taken care of me so far and I trust your judgment more than I do mine. What's next on the agenda?"

Almost every day, however, some little thing came up which was unexpected.

There was, for instance, the time when Dick, Sam, and I were sitting in the Whit-Craft having a coffee break.

Dick, who was seated by the window, looked out and suddenly exclaimed, "There's our Smith Craft drifting by!"

And, indeed, the Smith Craft had broken loose, was out in the middle of the channel, and was being swept along by the incoming tide, with a strong possibility that before we could recover it it would drift up to the shoal part of the river which was just above where we were camped.

264

If the boat stranded itself there at high tide we would really be in a predicament, because any boat we could have used for pursuit or rescue would have a greater draft and would have run aground long before we reached the Smith Craft.

Something had to be done and done fast.

Sam Hicks, who has instantaneous reactions, shot out of the Whit-Craft, over the plank to the shore, raced along the shore, got aboard the River Queen which was moored some forty yards away, picked up a rope, dashed out on the stern of the River Queen, and made himself a lasso.

Sam is an ex-cowboy, bronc stomper, calf roper, and general all-around cattleman.

It was a pleasure to see him work at high speed, fixing up a rope, forming a loop, and then throwing about thirty feet of rope in an accurate cast which fell directly over the bow of the drifting boat.

Sam Hicks throws an impromptu lasso to catch our Smith Craft before it drifts aground.

Then Sam gently—very gently—an inch at a time, started tightening the line so that it would catch on the metallic projection designed to hold a rope.

The trouble was that there was a rope already tied to this projection, a rope which was dragging in the water.

In view of the rising and falling tides we used stern anchors for the larger boats, but the Smith Craft was smaller and so we simply tied it up to the limber branch of an overhanging bush.

This branch had enough resiliency to rise and fall with tide, yet, at least theoretically, it had enough strength so it would hold the boat against the pull of the tide.

It now appeared that the tug of the tide had pulled the rope down the tapering limb, and the Smith Craft was loose.

Twice Sam made perfect casts with his line, and twice the rope slipped off without holding.

Then the boat was out of range of the line and there was a

We tied up the Valco cruiser between the two house cruisers.

mad scramble to get in the stern anchor on the Valco, to get the lines cast loose, the engine warmed up, and make a sprint to get to the Smith Craft before it grounded in shallow water.

The Valco literally knifed through the water, came alongside the Smith Craft, and Sam and Dick picked up the dragging rope with a boat hook and brought the Smith Craft back.

While it lasted, however, it was a nice bit of excitement.

For the most part, the days were all too short. Dick tried an occasional foray after salmon for half an hour at a time. We used the shallow draft boats to go way up the river, over the riffles and bars and into new waters.

And, of course, every day or so we would take a fast boat and go to Giusti's, stop in at the cool bar to have a draft beer, or one of "Lo's" wonderful Tom Collinses, then go up to Jerry Waterworth's Shell Station at Walnut Grove, pick up mail at the post office; go on to Locke and see our Chinese friends, Connie, Stanford, and George; replenish our supplies, return to Giusti's, pick up gasoline, drinking water, and ice.

Since we kept our generators running almost twenty-four hours a day, we had to haul in gasoline. And, while we did a little swimming, we relied mostly on the shower bath, which necessitated hauling in water.

These trips, however, were pleasant experiences during which we renewed our contacts with friends.

Occasionally, we would have barbecues out on the boat.

On one occasion, we even got Connie and Stanford King and George Marr to drive out to a place where they could park their car by a nearby drawbridge, where we picked them up with the Valco and whisked them into camp where we had a nice charcoal fire going in the barbecue grate. We put on thick steaks and had a glorious evening, topped off by a really wonderful pie Connie King had made from her own recipe.

This was toward the end of our stay and after we had discovered a place where it would be safe to park an automobile near the drawbridge. If we had only known that earlier, we would have been having a series of barbecues, because Sam is an expert steak broiler over charcoal and I love to sit around with friends and eat good juicy steaks.

The big trouble with the Delta country is that, since so many of the roads run along the tops of the levees, it is all but impossible to get a place where cars can be parked near the waterways. And, while we have powerful searchlights on the Valco, I dislike starting out at ten or eleven o'clock at night to take guests back along the winding waterways to Walnut Grove or Giusti's.

CHAPTER SIXTEEN

Until We Meet Again

Inevitably came the time when we simply had to get back. Dick DeShazer had to give a deposition in court, and I had to get the boats back into storage. "Doc" Lewis had to get to Los Angeles to attend a big convention; and there were a hundred and one details which needed personal attention.

So we got up early in the morning, packed up, put on the coffeepot, listened to Bill Bates and learned that it was going to be a perfect day in the Delta, untied the lines, hauled in the stern anchors, and were on our way.

In clear, warm, perfect Indian summer weather we brought our various boats into their berths by one-thirty in the afternoon.

We had time to go to the Chicken Shack for a cheeseburger; then Jean, "Doc" Lewis, Sam, and I drove back to Giusti's by the road along the levee. We picked up the car we had been keeping at Giusti's and the car "Doc" Lewis had rented in San Francisco and drove back to the house trailers.

The next day I rode into Oakland with "Doc" and got him started on the San Francisco Freeway. Sam Hicks followed us in one of our cars and brought me back. The next day we started south for my main office in Temecula.

The boats are up there in the berths at Bud Remsburg's

Marina. It is now too late in the season to go out and do much camping—that is, it is too late for me because if the so-called tule fog moved in on us I certainly wouldn't try to navigate in the Delta country.

These tule fogs are a peculiar phenomenon of the San Joaquin and Sacramento valleys. They take their names after the tules, a large reed of the bullrush family, towering perhaps six or seven feet out of the water, and which line many of the sloughs and channels in the Delta country.

The tule fog is a very fine-grained, very dense, white fog, which settles soundlessly upon the surface of the water and the adjacent land and stays and stays and stays.

A couple of hundred feet up, the sun will be shining with warmth, but down within the tule fog, the sunbeams cannot penetrate. The air has a milky color and the chill creeps into the very marrow of one's bones.

During times of tule fog there are all sorts of emergencies in the Delta country, numerous pile-ups of automobiles and a series of chain-reaction accidents on the highways in the San Joaquin and Sacramento valleys. Airports are closed for days at a time, and always that steady, silent fog blanketing the country day and night.

In the late fall and winter, however, we can go back to the Delta country and find many good days when we can go out for an afternoon of catfishing or just relaxing.

Those house cruisers are up there, filled with gasoline, with drinking water, hot and cold washing water, electricity at our fingertips, all ready to go.

We have only to unplug the electricity at the dock, start the motors, switch on the generators on the boats, and we are in business.

And the minute we get away from the dock we are living a new, carefree life.

The advantage of a houseboat is that the moment the lines are cast loose the new world takes over. The yachtsman

270

doesn't have to go anyplace in particular in order to be there. He is already there, surrounded by all the familiar conveniences and luxuries, ready to tie up in some secluded cove, read, sleep, fish, or, if he wants to, watch a football game on television. He can listen to other boats on the ship-to-shore radio. He can find shade on the forward deck or sunshine on the afterdeck, or, if he wants, he can stretch out for a sunbath on the sundeck.

The world is his oyster.

I can leave the hectic atmosphere of my Temecula headquarters, jump in a car and, eight hours later, be aboard my house cruisers, having made the transition from the volume of work, the constantly ringing telephones, the stress and strain of meeting deadlines, to the peaceful isolation of the house trailers at DeShazer's Trailer Park and the relaxed atmosphere of the house cruisers—balm to jangled nerves.

And always throughout the Delta is that warm friendship, that atmosphere of a community which has kept aloof from the rush of commercialism, the hustle and bustle of bumper-to-bumper traffic.

The hundreds of miles of inland waterways sparkle in the sunlight. Friends have a cheery smile and a warm greeting.

The world of water is a world of relaxation and friendship.

A Note About the Author
ERLE STANLEY GARDNER

Erle Stanley Gardner was born in Malden, Massachusetts and raised in Massachusetts, Oregon and California. He studied law briefly at Valparaiso University in Indiana, but gained the majority of his knowledge studying law in law offices. He was admitted to the California bar at age twenty-one. After nine years of spare-time writing and practicing law, he gave up his legal work and became a full-time writer. His first Perry Mason novel, *The Case of the Velvet Claws*, was published in 1932, and has been followed by 77 others. Mr. Gardner is also the author of 26 books written under the pseudonym A. A. Fair. GYPSY DAYS ON THE DELTA is his 10th non-fiction book. Mr. Gardner lives on a ranch in Southern California.